International Business in
the Middle East

Other Titles in This Series

Westview Special Studies in International Economics and Business

International Business in the Middle East: Case Studies
edited by Ashok Kapoor

Many of the failures of foreign companies operating in the Middle East have had their origins in problems of attitude and lack of preparation rather than in difficulties with the area's characteristic business environment. The case studies in this book reveal that few foreign companies prepare adequately for project development and implementation. The authors discuss several dimensions of business development in the Middle East, identifying distinguishing features of the region, but also recommending that foreign companies use their experiences in other developing areas—especially in Asia—as a guide. They call for particular attention to the human resources needs of an operation and the special requirements of host governments. The book is designed for both the academic and business communities.

Ashok Kapoor is professor of marketing and international business at New York University and founder of The International Negotiation Institute. He has pioneered in the development of the negotiation exercise for training, problem solving, and research. Dr. Kapoor is the author of several publications and also advises public and private organizations.

This study is the result of a project
sponsored and administered by the
Fund for Multinational Management Education

International Business in the Middle East: Case Studies

edited by Ashok Kapoor

Contributors:
Eugene Bird
Gary E. Lloyd
John Seifert
Ibrahim F. I. Shihata
William Stoever

Westview Press/Boulder, Colorado

Westview Special Studies in International Economics and Business

Copyright © 1979 by Westview Press, Inc.

Published in 1979 in the United States of America by
   Westview Press, Inc.
   5500 Central Avenue
   Boulder, Colorado 80301
   Frederick A. Praeger, Publisher

Library of Congress Cataloging in Publication Data
Kapoor, Ashok, 1940–
   International business in the Middle East.
   Bibliography: p.
   1. Corporations, Foreign—Near East—Case studies. 2. Investments, Foreign—Near East—Case studies.   3. International business enterprises—Case studies.
I. Title.
HD2891.9.K36   658.4   78-15414
ISBN 0-89158-257-6

Printed and bound in the United States of America

Contents

Foreword

A lasting international business relationship is conditioned by the extent to which the business and government participants understand the context in which each functions. *International Business in the Middle East* illustrates the importance for foreign companies of understanding political, economic, and cultural characteristics of the Middle East, and the importance for host country officials and institutions of recognizing the constraints on foreign companies in operations undertaken in the Middle East.

The seven case studies presented in this work refer specifically to foreign business endeavors in the Middle East and to Middle Eastern investment in other countries. However, the characteristics of business development and the approach to negotiating for a lasting business relationship highlighted here are relevant for business and government officials in other parts of the world.

The publication of *International Business in the Middle East* is an example of the continuing work of the Fund for Multinational Management Education in promoting dialogue between private and public sector groups for more effective and responsive policy formation.

Henry R. Geyelin
President

Preface

Except for the extractive sector, the international company has historically had a very limited presence in the Middle East. However, since the early 1970s, and in particular after the increase of crude oil prices, a vast number of companies have descended upon the Middle East. The experiences of companies and host countries in dealing with each other provide general observations that can be useful to corporate and governmental officials formulating policies and operational plans. This book highlights some of those experiences by reviewing efforts by foreign companies to develop business relationships in the Middle East. Through a series of case studies, we are able to interpret business developments in the Middle East from several points of view. Interpretation from the standpoint of negotiations is emphasized in Chapter 1 and in some of the guideline questions provided for each case. The case studies also highlight aspects of decision-making processes and the interactions between foreign companies and private and public host-country organizations.

The book does not deal with foreign investment rules and regulations or provide macroeconomic information, nor does it purport to be an investment guide or a source of factual information. References in the bibliography cover many of these topics.

Chapter 1 offers characteristics of international business

development and negotiation in the Middle East. Chapters 2 through 8 present seven case studies that reflect business development in various sectors such as industrial goods, housing and construction, services, automotive parts, fertilizer production, and real estate development.

The size of the companies included in the cases, as determined by volume of sales, ranges from small to large. The small and medium-sized companies have typically sought a sales representation agreement in the Middle East. Equity investments, if accepted at all, are mainly undertaken by large companies. Nearly half of the cases describe efforts of companies to establish a presence in one or more Middle Eastern markets. Two cases deal with the efforts to implement a project; one case presents a program for expansion of operations. Geographically, the cases focus on the countries of the Gulf.

The cases highlight several oversights of companies in understanding the business environment of the Middle East and the correct approach to negotiating a lasting business relationship. Some of the oversights are:

1. an inadequate knowledge of the host country and preparation for in-country operations;
2. an insufficient allocation of time to projects by senior management, especially at the initial stage of entry into a country;
3. an inadequate recognition that the areas and scope of assistance sought by the local affiliate (agent, representative, partner) will be significantly different from the company's definition of what is fair, reasonable, required, and legally stated;
4. an insufficient awareness of the critical role of the local affiliate in a company's growth prospects in a host country;
5. advocacy or acceptance of an unrealistic time framework for the achievement of targets;

6. poor understanding of the importance of effective relationships with powerful local groups and individuals
   for efficient business operations;
7. a failure to recognize fully the importance of trust in
   personal and professional relationships; and
8. insufficient attention to building a management team
   (often composed of diverse nationalities) capable of
   functioning effectively in an environment largely
   unfamiliar to many, if not all, of the team members.

The cases can be used for courses in international business,
in area studies curricula, and for executive programs. The
pedagogy can be both case discussion and simulations.

The questions and issues raised by the cases emphasize
four areas:

1. adequacy of the approach to business development in
   the Middle East being used by a company;
2. characteristics of negotiation displayed by various
   parties and the relationship of the characteristics to
   the particular business environment of which they
   are a part;
3. specific programs of action for achieving objectives; and
4. changes of attitudes, personnel and structures, both internal and external to an organization, to facilitate
   achieving objectives.

Additional research is urgently required on all areas of international business in the Middle East in order to assist decision-
makers in corporations and governments in formulating and
implementing policies and operational plans. Specific areas
for further research include:

- analyzing the experiences of international companies
  and host developing countries (particularly in Asia) for
  their relevance to the Middle East;

- investigating the role of the international company in promoting multiparty projects in third countries involving at least one or more international companies, one or more Middle Eastern parties, and one or more host country parties; and
- developing more case studies with a focus on the international company and host governments.

Without the cooperation of companies and host countries this book would not have been possible. A number of individuals have helped in the formulation and completion of this book; in keeping with their preference, however, most of them remain anonymous. The Fund for Multinational Management Education provided financial support for this study, and over the years it has facilitated research in the general area of negotiations. The Graduate School of Business Administration of New York University facilitated this work through released time and overall support for research in negotiations. The authors of the various case studies have taken time from their extremely busy schedules to reflect on their broad experiences.

Ashok Kapoor

About the Contributors

Ashok Kapoor is professor of marketing and international business at New York University and founder of The International Negotiation Institute. He has pioneered in the development of the negotiation exercise for training, problem solving, and research. Dr. Kapoor is the author of several publications, including *Strategy and Negotiation for the International Corporation* (with John Fayerweather), *International Business-Government Communications* (with Jack Behrman and Jean Boddewyn), and *Planning for International Business Negotiations*. In addition, Dr. Kapoor advises public and private organizations.

Eugene Bird served as a foreign service officer for the U.S. Department of State from 1956 to 1975 in Middle Eastern posts from Jerusalem, Beirut, and Cairo, to Saudi Arabia and the Gulf. His specialty is economics, with special emphasis on the impact of the new oil economies. He is now International Trade Director for the governors of Oregon, Idaho, and Washington, operating under the Pacific Northwest Regional Commission. He has also served as a visiting professor at the University of Oregon and Oregon State University, and is consultant to several multinational corporations.

Gary E. Lloyd is the Director of the BCIU Institute (Business Council for International Understanding) of the American University in Washington, D.C. The institute trains personnel and their families to cope and function more effectively overseas. Mr. Lloyd has taught at the Graduate School of Business Administration of the University of Southern California. He is a member of the editorial board of *International Dimension* of the American Assembly of Collegiate Schools of Business and the Academy of International Business, and he co-founded the Society for Intercultural Education, Training, and Research.

John Seifert is a graduate of Princeton University in Middle Eastern politics and language and New York University's Graduate School of Business Administration in international management. He has lived and worked for seven years with a local national utility and an international corporation in a number of Middle Eastern countries. He is particularly experienced in the development of financial operations and the application of American and European management systems in that area. Mr. Seifert is currently a member of the international corporate banking staff at J. Henry Schroder Bank and Trust Company in New York.

Dr. Ibrahim F. I. Shihata is at present Director-General of the OPEC Special Fund. He was educated in Egypt and in the United States, and was awarded a doctorate of Juridical Science from Harvard University. Dr. Shihata has consulted for governments and international agencies, served as general counsel and senior advisor of the Kuwait Fund for Arab Economic Development, actively participated in the creation of many international financial institutions especially in the Middle East, and taught at Ain-Shams University in Egypt. He is also a prolific writer with several books and articles to his credit.

William Stoever is an assistant professor of international business and law at Rutgers Graduate School of Business Administration in Newark, New Jersey. He holds a J.D. from Harvard Law School and a Ph.D. in international management from New York University. He has spent seven years overseas as a teacher, student, and traveler, visiting ninety countries in Africa, Asia, Europe, and Latin America. His primary research interests are the economic, legal, planning, and negotiating problems of multinational investment in less developed countries.

1
International Business Development and Negotiations: Selected Characteristics of the Middle East

Eugene Bird

Selected Characteristics

To be really successful in the Middle East, in business just as in diplomacy, requires an understanding of the Middle Eastern negotiator. So much has been written and spoken since 1973 on both the Arab countries and Iran as unique markets that it is difficult to sort myth from reality.

Recently *L'Express,* not noted for a pro–Middle East bias, had a two-page spread with a full-page picture of an Arab in his typical *kefiyah* looking suspiciously intelligent. *"Pratiquez-vous aussi bien que lui l'art de la negociation?"* asked the headline. (Are you as good at negotiating as he is?) The advertisement was by a French bank, Société Générale, which, in comparison to American banks, has done little business in the Middle East itself, but is important in the North African trade, where the French learned much of what they know about Arabs.

"Shrewdness, finesse, ability, a taste for secrecy, patience, self-control, perfect knowledge of the files; it took the recent oil crisis to reveal to the stunned Western world the extraordinary talents of Arab negotiators." This is an exaggeration, of course, but it represents the revised appraisal of the Arab going on all over the Western world. The need now is for a controlled response to our new view of the Arab as a business

negotiator. While many advantages do lie with him, he is in
need of Western ties; he is basically imaginative, yet conserva-
tive, and has the same need as every other business negotiator,
that is, to avoid being made a fool by accepting less than the
optimum.

Are there any unique facets to negotiation with Middle
Easterners? It is tempting simply to look at the Middle East
as a whole, as if it were a single, large marketplace. But it is
much more than that, and is becoming as diverse as Europe
was in the nineteenth and early twentieth centuries. Negotiating with Kuwait may resemble negotiating with a Swiss
banker, except that the woman negotiator is already evident
in Kuwait. The Saudis, the quietest of the Arabs, are easily
underrated by both their fellow Arabs and by Westerners.
Iranians are flamboyant in their style, promising sometimes
more than they can deliver, and are very specific and know-
ledgeable in their demands. Before discussing differences
among Middle Eastern negotiators, however, it may be useful
to review cultural similarities endemic to all groups in the area.

The generation gap is not a Western phenomenon. The
head of the Middle Eastern firm may have little more than a
superficial acquaintance with the West; but his son, nephew,
or general manager may share with many an American negotiator allegiance to the same U.S. alma mater and fondness
for the hamburger. A leading U.S. engineering firm, faced
with simultaneous negotiation with three Arab nationalities
on a single project (an increasingly common kind of negotiation), evaluated the Saudi engineers as the best they had seen.
They should be—the company's own engineers were graduates
of the same universities as the Saudis.

A sense of humor about oneself certainly does not harm
the chances of achieving a breakthrough in tough Middle
East negotiations. During difficult negotiations between
Aramco and the Saudi government some years ago, a two-
stage system emerged. The experts would meet and talk ex-
haustively, coming to no agreement during the day. The two

principals would meet in the evening, often on the way to the airport in Minister of Petroleum and Mineral Resources Yamani's Mercedes. The confrontations of the day would be reviewed briefly and the knottiest problem usually solved. On one of these occasions during the month-long negotiations, the Aramco vice-president turned to Yamani and said, "We have taken care of all the elephants. Now let us deal with the rabbits." Sheik Yamani laughed and repeated the story to friends, adding, "That is where the profits were for Aramco . . . with the rabbits."

One should not be surprised, however, to find as well surprising sophistication among Middle Eastern negotiators. Yamani himself is a classic example of this point. Shortly after three or four Saudis had been trained by Aramco in computer science technology and had taken positions with the Ministry of Petroleum and Mineral Resources, Yamani and his staff met the Aramco negotiators at a Lebanese mountain resort. To each proposed change in oil price and lifting arrangements, Yamani produced his own figures, independent of the company figures. He had installed his own small computer center and manned it with his Aramco-trained experts.

The atmosphere of the negotiations is especially important in the Middle East. Yamani is reported to have made a habit of opening negotiations with a series of unrelated questions: "What is happening in Iran? Is that man in Libya still giving you a bad time?" As one executive noted, Yamani knew more about the Iranian and Libyan scenes than did the Americans, and his questions were more directed at setting the mood for negotiations than at soliciting information.

It is extremely important to the Middle Eastern negotiator to have a confident feeling about the character and personality of those with whom he negotiates. It is usually necessary to prepare the way by sharing social occasions, developing friendships, and revealing early and with good proportion and dignity "what is behind your mind."

Frequently the Middle Eastern executive demands more personal involvement in briefing than would the Westerner. When a company asked permission to send a group to brief Yamani's experts on what was expected to happen in oil offtake and supply, he expressed an interest in being present himself. The executive joked, "Of course, Zaki, we will arrange a time convenient for you, but you won't take the time . . . I know that." Yamani protested that he would, and he did. The American had used a sense of humor, coupled with the Arab sense of honor, to make Yamani want to keep his word. While it can be effective, such a technique must be natural and used very sparingly.

Negotiations are long if there are any complexities at all. The Middle Easterner who feels at an advantage may politely request proposals from the other side. The question then becomes whether one should respond with an outrageously high bid and make a request for concessions that are obviously inflated. According to oil company negotiators, this is not the best tactic. It is better to explain quietly and rationalize terms by some logical device that will stand up and at least initially or nominally impress the other side. Fencing, not bushwhacking, tactics are called for. Adroit arguments, not high demands, impress the Arab. The Arabic language itself places a high value on clever logic and shrewd appraisal. Direct confrontations may occasionally be necessary, but then they are best done with humor and through softening devices that signal to the other party that this particular demand is a must in the negotiations.

Experienced negotiators have found that though the discussion may become quite specific, final details are often deferred and are dependent upon the general agreement. The wrap-up may take place only at the last minute, literally while the pens are being prepared for the signatures.

It has been found that negotiations are pursued in an entirely different manner when a technical or nonroyal minister, rather than a member of the royal family, is the negotiator. The technocrat will be much more likely to insist on specifics and demonstrate a knowledge of Western concepts of finance, marketing, and administrative techniques. In the negotiating situation, however, he will still seek a personal relationship of trust.

Recently, an important authorization was given a deputy to a national bank to negotiate with an American advisory service. The highly trained, but young, Saudi financier faced representatives of the American firm and a young prince who had made the initial arrangements. The talks seemed aimless for several days. The Americans discovered by accident that the Arab bank representative was highly suspicious of the presence of the Arab intermediary in the talks. "We do not want anyone with a vested interest in these talks except the Americans," the negotiator finally admitted in private. The talks proceeded smoothly after the intermediary was gently removed.

The profile for a perfect negotiator includes frankness, quick-wittedness, calmness, sensitivity, a finely tuned sense of dignity and grace, and a generous sense of humor. A negotiator must occasionally endure flamboyant behavior and be able to genuinely appreciate and relate to the closeness of entangled family life in the Middle East. Above all, he must present a sincere and open mind.

Corporate Profiles in Approaches to Negotiation

The variety of corporate images that have proven successful in the Middle Eastern market proves the diversity of successful methods of negotiation. Most well-regarded corporations, however, seem to be discreet, underplaying their role in joint operations. They are usually global in their marketing span, but are at the same time able to delegate rather comprehensive and direct authority to their local Middle Eastern field managers, while insisting on constant feedback and modern management techniques. That impresses both Arabs and

Iranians, particularly when it proves profitable.

The approach used by a few corporations coming to the market in the Middle East includes protective phalanxes of vice-presidents, experts, computer programmers, jets standing by—a sort of panoply of overwhelming arrogancies. Others approach it in cowboy boots and suede jackets—informalities that appall trained area experts. Although these negotiators may be amusing to Middle Easterners, they also have proven to be competent in their discussions and successful in securing contracts.

A third type of corporate approach is the use of the old school tie, the friend, the man who has been successful in his own corporation and decides to exploit his friendship of years gone by with a Middle Easterner who has now risen to a ranking role in his own society. The U.S. corporation may elevate its man to vice-president or director of international marketing (Middle East), regardless of his age or background. Successful negotiation in the Middle East may result in relocation of the new executive to Athens, Bahrain, Riyadh, Cairo, or Tehran, close to the location of decision-making authority. Sometimes the old school tie works, sometimes it does not. However, unless the new vice-president has the extra patience and persistence to pursue more than the old school friend, he is not likely to succeed in doing anything more than spending an unusually large amount of his corporation's money.

One large eastern institution with close ties to a Middle Eastern prince sent a five-man old-school-tie contingent seeking financial support for a new chair in Middle East studies and other programs. While not entirely shunned, they were politely told that during the time the minister-prince had been at the institution, he had been constantly reminded of his Arab ancestry in a rather derogatory fashion and he did not consider the present university administration any different from that of his time. Such frank talk from an Arab is unusual.

Summing Up

During one six-week period in early 1975, the U.S. Embassy in Jidda recorded forty different bankers or banking groups seeking advice on making the Saudi connection. The number of other American firms was not recorded, but as bankers tend to follow businessmen in investigating investment opportunities, we can assume that the forty banking groups were preceded by at least as many business groups. In these circumstances it is understandable that the number of seminars and books on the Middle East market have burgeoned.

It is worth listening to new information about the Middle East. However, it would be foolish to follow any of it blindly, without testing against the key to negotiations, which demands that accords be beneficial for all parties. An intriguing blend of grace and intelligence keyed to that rule is what makes the Middle East such an interesting and unique market. The following illustrations elaborate on the characteristics that affect international business negotiations there.

1. Corporate Personalities and Personal Relationships

Shaw represented Corporation Y, a company specializing in an area of airport landing systems. Smaller than most, the corporation recruited Shaw for the specific job of carving out a share of the rapidly expanding market in a country where Shaw had as his closest contact the man most responsible for airport works. It took Shaw many months to overcome the competition, both American and foreign, but the company backed him in his efforts and before the end of a year the first contract was ready for signature.

By the time the contract was written, a vice-president at headquarters had been placed in charge. He arranged to be present and actually signed the contract that Shaw had formulated. By the end of the second year, additional contracts were in the offing and again the vice-president magically appeared and got his name on the contracts. Although the vice-president stayed in the limelight at company headquarters, Shaw knew that he had absolutely no standing in the country or with Shaw's friends. Petty disagreements between the field and headquarters increased. Shaw was suddenly pulled away and replaced by the vice-president. Local sources predicted that the company would get little additional business, not because it transferred Shaw, but because of the way it was done.

This example demonstrates that corporate politics are sometimes more oriental than those of the Middle East. Host country nationals will do business with people they know.

2. Persistence

John Z. was the son of the founder of a small road-building firm interested in opening business in the Arab world. He had no experience there, but was able to quickly ingratiate himself in the society partly because the Arabs understood completely his role as a son in the corporation, and partly because of his youth and natural dignity. The company was doing less than $10 million a year in business, but its programs at home were winding down and it sought an expanding and less competitive market abroad. The effort cost the company at least $10,000 a month and went on for more than a year before the company even placed among the top three bidders. Finally, nearly eighteen months after first arriving, John Z. won a bid on a relatively small but potentially very profitable contract for fifty kilometers of road to be built to full American specifications. But the war of 1973 came before the contract could be finally negotiated and signed. John Z. had excellent rapport with the ministry and asked to see the minister when it became clear that the American company would not receive the contract. The minister told him that he could not award such a contract to an American firm at that time. "But wait," he said, "don't go away." The wait extended for another eight months, but the contract was eventually signed after a new figure was negotiated. The company continued to prosper with additional contracts.

Bidding is not a rigid process with Arab governments in particular and even less so with private Arab corporations. The personal affection and esteem with which the company representative was viewed added very little advantage in the negotiations over price and terms. However, it was certainly the critical element during the crisis in the contract negotiation.

3. Big Man in the Middle East

Corporation C was very hungry to move into the Middle East in a combined construction and servicing contract. As it was also convinced that the first contract would not be the last, it wanted to establish a firm hold in the area and cut its bid substantially below the competition for a big project involving complex training schedules. The company won the contract and then had to agree to tight timing to keep it. The company searched for a Middle East expert and found a retired businessman in Alaska who supposedly had outstanding credentials. He was big, heavy, and bearded, and he fit exactly the image most of the vice-presidents had of the typical Middle East executive who could handle the tough problems of cutting through the Arab red tape. Corporation C hired him without checking into why he had left the Middle East in the first place. The corporation delivered everything the man wanted, including a grand piano for his wife and a fine villa with swimming pool.

He seemed to start strongly, recruiting personnel away from several other companies and paying top dollar for experienced employees in language and special training— the real key to the contract. The staff may have expanded too rapidly, because regular employees sent out to assist him from corporate headquarters began to complain that no records were being kept and that there was little effort at management of any kind, much less the modern control necessary for a complex multimillion dollar operation. There were even reports that he abused certain employees. Some quit, and the training program ground down. The government began to hold up payments due. A controller sent out by headquarters waded through masses of complaints but also got into trouble and had to be removed. Vice-presidents began dropping in more frequently in an effort to negotiate with the ministry.

Bankers began pressing the company and the cash flow deteriorated beyond the most pessimistic predictions. That triggered the arrival of Corporation C's chairman, who promptly removed the manager and stayed on for three long weeks in an attempt to correct deficiencies in the operation. He later described these three weeks as the most difficult of his life. The contract was almost cancelled, and the company lost two other good opportunities for further work. This is an example of the consequences of failing to monitor corporate decisions—in this instance the hiring of the Alaska businessman. It took two more changes in command and a further shakeup at headquarters before the company got back on the track.

Area and language-trained experts are absolutely essential, but they should be treated as ordinary recruits. The appetite of this large company for business made it lose sight of the operating goal, which is to make a profit without losing a reputation for excellence.

4. When a Firm Price Is Always Negotiable

Corporation G, a European multinational, was well established in country A and was pushing for a $400-million contract. The project had been American-designed, the project director was American-educated, and most of the similar projects in the country had been American-built. There was sharp competition from the best European, Japanese, and American firms. Company G, with its own government solidly behind it, chose the strategy of preparing a firm bid price as required by the tender with the possibility of further negotiations if there were any engineering changes. Such changes were almost a certainty because of technological developments already in the works.

The Americans, by contrast, decided to require an escalation clause that made their firm bid meaningless. Even so, they were offered the project if they would agree to a "firm bid" $60 million higher than Corporation G's. The Americans insisted on the escalation clause. Even when warned that they were about to lose the bid, they refused to write an agreeably vague engineering change clause that would allow the officials to save face. European Corporation G did win the contract. Due to engineering changes, the price escalated far beyond any prediction at the time of the bid. One notes with some irony that much of the procurement for the project has come from America anyway, partly because the dollar goods are cheaper with devaluation. One of the American bidders went on to win another major contract, but in a contention that is not really valid, continues to blame its loss of the first one on foreign government pressures.

This example points out that corporate inflexibility does make for real losses and baffles the Middle Easterners rooting for American involvement because of their own respect for American technology and their own American attachments. Home government pressures may occasionally be helpful in assuring fair competition, but home government "inquiries" to place pressure on Middle Eastern governments are no substitute for corporate flexibility.

5. Consulting a Consultant

The industrial development division of a major company in the Middle East employed for many years a bright American industrial engineer whose main job was to encourage local corporations to create joint ventures and provide services for the large company, and to work closely with local merchants and competent Western firms. By agreement with the company, the engineer eventually spun himself off and set up a consulting organization with four local partners. The initial venture into a $5-million chemical plant was neatly executed and more quickly completed than if it had been done in the United States.

Subsequent efforts in several other fields including construction were equally successful and the firm continued to prosper, expanding into joint support for a major electronic project. The key to success appeared to derive from the competence of the original engineer and a careful day-to-day following of the local scene. The consultant group, which by now expanded to employ five men in various fields from several countries, seemed to know better than anyone else how to corral local investors for soundly based immediate return projects and contracts. The profile was kept low, expenses were carefully monitored, and good management techniques were used without assaulting the entire family corporation-based structure of local business.

Local business was just emerging from a tradition of merchant mentality, quick turnover, and shortage-based pricing. Give and take between the two business cultures was kept within reasonable bounds and difficulties were negotiated before they loomed large. The consultant group participated in each of the stages of the projects and acted as confidant for both sides.

A graduated and realizable growth, goal-based program was almost unwittingly adopted, and pragmatism and acceptance of different approaches to solve problems to accommodate each partner characterized decisions. When production schedules for critical components for the first plant fell behind and use of an expensive but long-range economical 747 was proposed at substantial additional cost, the idea was

approved without hesitation by the board of directors because of confidence in the individual who founded the consulting company.

Everyone agreed on the reliability and the cost conscious-
ness of the Westerner and they readily followed his sugges-
tions. He was in turn believed by the Western clients as good
for his word, and his views on the local situation were credible.
He often pointed out that, because his partners were from
several different families, they would be unlikely to gang up
on the foreign shareholders in any joint venture operation.

In the Middle East, it is best to find persons who have continuous contacts with local entrepreneurs, yet who do not
appear to represent only themselves or a salient figure in the
local hierarchy. Too often, agents cannot introduce an investor to the centers of power and real decision within the
government, and are ignored, though politely received, in the
private sector. A careful check of the credentials of inter-
mediaries is essential, for, while they are often highly useful,
they will never make an impractical or overpriced scheme fly.

6. Ethics and a Professional Planning Group

One of the most prestigious country planning contracts in
the world had been awarded to Company XYZ, which
drafted the Middle East country's first five-year plan and was
hired to monitor the plan with a substantial staff. While
relations had always been difficult in terms of details, the
XYZ planning staff was highly motivated and the contract
had been quite profitable, permitting the planning group to
operate in other countries and with companies interested in
certain Middle East markets.

The first plan was simplistic, but when the company was
awarded the planning contract for the second five-year plan
and began work on it, a pledge was extracted from the
government that it would be a truly professional job with
high standards based on careful economic and statistical

evaluations. For more than a year, the company conducted a careful analysis of the plan. Only in the defense area was it hazy and incomplete, which bothered no one. In key civilian agencies, the planners found an amazing degree of cooperation, and the key advisors and officials trained in Western systems approach were allowed for once to define realistic programs. A total figure of several billion dollars beyond actual spending in the first plan was quoted as the new plan spending target. The initial plan outline hinted that any surplus funds would be channelled into a tightly held investment plan separate from the main development plan.

Suddenly, because of pressures from the cabinet, the decision was made that the plan should remain intact as the foreign technicians and their well-trained local counterparts had determined, but that the cost of the plan should be arbitrarily tripled.

The cabinet felt threatened because the publicly admitted existence of very large surplus funds was an economic problem that had both domestic and international impact. The planning group had to decide whether or not this was the moment simply to claim professional ethics were involved and walk away or to help the planning minister and triple the costs shown in the plan document. The ultimate decision to triple the costs was rationalized on the basis that so long as the plan document was left intact, and since the costing was becoming slightly speculative in view of world inflation, the tripling of the costs as shown could be explained away as politically and socially necessary.

The changes were made, to the continuing puzzlement of everyone using the document, and the planning group remained to monitor the plan itself with a reduced staff.

The concept of professionalism is important but has less application in areas like the Middle East where power and politics are ruled by never having to admit a fact when face can be saved. Professionalism must occasionally be rationalized, though this does not necessarily mean compromised.

7. Negotiating the Nitty Gritty

John represented a large construction company with some experience in the Middle East which hoped to convince a Middle Eastern government that the present environment demanded cost-plus-fixed-fee or incentive-fee contract arrangements. The company had lost money or had only minimal profits on a rising number of contracts in nearby countries. All attempts to persuade the government contracting teams that they would be able to save both money and negotiating effort by adopting a more flexible approach in the face of inflationary pressures had failed. The company was torn between wanting to continue and threatening to withdraw from future bidding on contracts unless changes were made.

John talked at length with both U.S. and British embassy officers with long experience in negotiating with the local government. He concluded that while a few lower-ranking officials might regret the departure of the company, the government bureaucracy would remain largely unmoved by any threat—and in fact might not only ignore but actually discourage any change.

The company had always entered projects with only a few local partners. John felt that any change in bidding terms must be worked out by common negotiation with the government by a cross section of both local and foreign companies. He even recommended that his company seek a joint venture partner, inevitable in the long run, and use the possibility of that as bait to encourage the government to make a step-by-step change. Beginning with certain allowable cost overruns permitted to be written into the contract, the change would be tied to some indexes that would be easily agreed to. Rises in the price of oil would not be acceptable since this would make for difficulties with the company's home government. It was also sensitive to using oil as a base with its host government.

John finally chose a series of basic supplies, including the price of private venture stevedores at the ports and the cost of cement and transport of it to the site. He then chose to take his figures with what they would mean to the economy in net savings as against inflated contract bidding, and presented them to a government minister known for his brash approach to such matters. The minister was known to be having trouble with completion of some contracts bid in too low. He saw a way by which he could solve his own ministry's problem and at the same time advance his own personal cause.

The figures were revised and translated by the minister into a proposal to the cabinet. After several weeks, and some further adroit presentations to other ministers sympathetic to the idea, a subcabinet committee was appointed to look into contract changes. The friendly minister was the chairman. The subcommittee reported back and not only urged adoption of an index system but also suggested authorization of cost-plus contracts even outside the defense establishment (which had used them) for a few exceptional cases. Though the cabinet failed to respond as the minister hoped, there did seem to be evidence in the cabinet of a new awareness of the contract problems.

The company was encouraged by the movement towards recognizing the problem and chose to bid in the next contract at a fixed fee but with an alternate lower estimate that amounted to a bid to include exactly what the subcommittee had recommended for escalation purposes.

Dealing with Middle East governments, except for the occasional resort to special agents' fees, is not unlike dealing with any government. It requires considerable numbers of carefully cultivated friendships and a logical approach to the problem.

8. Divorcing an Agent

Company S was a major exporter of potato products. It

had made a few sales to Saudi Arabia, mostly for the Westerners living there. The company had used an agent for the Dhahran/Aramco oil area and a separate one for Jidda, a thousand miles away. The business had grown very fast after 1973, even outside the foreign community areas, with the introduction of fast-food operations and supermarkets. The company recognized that the two agents, though nominally not in head-to-head competition, did overlap in their areas. In fact, each pressed hard to become the company's exclusive agent. A possible interpretation in fact could be placed on the original agreements, giving both "exclusive" right to selling the product for the whole kingdom. The company discussed its plight with commercial sources, including the U.S. Embassy, but reached no conclusion. Company S felt that it would have trouble regardless of the agent it chose.

The vice-president in charge of international sales decided formally to ignore the problem and continue to deal with both Saudi business houses. The vice-president felt the problem might be resolved by expansion in the market if communication could be kept open with both parties. He wanted to explore the possibility of an informal arrangement between the two agents, and decided to travel there on a special trip to explore the markets with both agents.

In Jidda he found both agents awaiting him with competing dinner invitations. The American company had anticipated this and had arranged for its own reception on neutral ground to which all the important supermarket customers and others were invited. The two agents were given prominent positions in the reception line. They were, of course, old friends, but did not refrain from competing for the frozen potato business that suddenly had such great potential.

Each tried to outbid the other for larger orders from the company and to plead his case for being named exclusive agent. The vice-president turned their requests aside by saying that he was only exploring the future of the market and would determine later what they would do about representation. But before he left, he jokingly accused both men of preparing to gang up on him. They laughed and the evening ended with promises from both to enter new large orders.

Later during the trip, special representatives of both agents appeared with heavy new orders for frozen and processed products. The vice-president concluded that he could nominate both men as co-agents and they would continue with the company without real objection. This is exactly what he did, and he felt he had been wise to explore the problem face to face.

He felt that any lesson in this derived from treating the agents as important human beings, while giving them no opportunity to challenge the right of the company to choose its agents, and by permitting both to gain face in front of their own business community and customers.

It is very difficult in the Middle East to find a divorce method that will not endanger an account and possibly have negative impact on potential accounts. Generally, the more dependent the agent (meaning in most instances the smaller he is), the more difficult the divorce will be unless the method has been specified in the original agreement.

2
Bangor Engineering Ltd.: Working with an Agent

Ashok Kapoor

This case study presents the attempt of a relatively small Australian company to appoint an agent and retain an employee to develop the Iranian market. The company experienced many severe problems in entering the Iranian market, primarily because it did not do its homework before and during its business endeavors in Iran. Factors contributing to the company's failure in Iran include the following: (1) It has grossly overestimated the ease of entry into the market. (2) Senior management has not allocated sufficient resources, especially in terms of management time, to allow for a meaningful effort to enter the market. (3) It has not been careful in selecting a local agent familiar with the local environment who can deal effectively with its characteristics. (4) It has not understood the absolute requirement of careful selection and training of its representative in Iran. (5) It has not understood that the areas and scope of assistance sought by the agent will be far greater than what is deemed to be fair, just, reasonable, or contractually provided for by the company. (6) It has tended to be condescending when dealing with host country nationals.

Unfortunately, the mistakes made by Bangor Engineering (BE) have been repeated far too often by many companies both large and small, especially in the Middle East. And it is difficult to correct a damaged image.

As you read this case, keep in mind the following issues: the specific course of action McBain should pursue if Bangor Engineering is to become successful in Iran in twenty-four months, the type and amount of resources McBain must commit to have a reasonable chance of success in Iran and other Gulf countries, and the specific changes Bangor Engineering must make in its Australian operations to improve its performance in Iran.

* * *

Bangor Engineering (BE) had $10 million in sales volume in portable cement mixers in Australia. The company was interested in the Middle East and had taken initial steps to position itself in Iran. In 1973 it had air-freighted a cement mixer to Tehran from Australia for a trade fair. McBain and Hawkins, two senior executives of BE, attended the trade fair and received several inquiries about the cement mixer.

McBain was an entrepreneur seeking rapid profits in the short term. He felt that the Middle East offered growth prospects greater than those in any other region of the world. In discussions with local construction firms at the trade fair, he received the distinct impression that a considerable amount of business could be developed in Iran and that money would not be a problem due to the greatly increased oil revenues. He was excited by investment potential in Iran and the Middle East in general, and before leaving the trade fair, he appointed Astra, a wholly European-owned company that handled the products of European manufacturers, as the local distributor for the cement mixer. The management of the company was extremely weak and consisted of older generation Europeans who had been in Iran for a long period in partnership with non-Muslim Iranians. However, despite these limitations, Astra had a better reputation than local companies for delivering what it promised. BE and Astra concluded an informal agreement and were to sign a formal agreement after a twelve-month trial period.

In the year following the appointment of Astra, McBain and Hawkins made two one-day stops in Tehran on their way to and from Europe. During these visits and as a result of publicity about major construction projects announced by the government, McBain in particular became infatuated with the seemingly unlimited business prospects in the Middle East. A good performance in the Middle East, largely reflected in immediate profits, would greatly improve McBain's position in the parent company.

However, BE had serious problems with entering the Iranian market: (1) It did not have any personnel with experience in the Middle East. (2) It did not have executives who were either qualified or willing to spend much time in the Middle East. (3) It had limited and generally unreliable information on market characteristics and selling requirements in the Middle East. (4) It was not in a financial position to undertake any significant financial investment to gain a foothold in the Middle East. (5) It faced internal management problems, including the resignation of several key executives.

Despite these restraints, BE was caught up in the general mood in Australia at the time, which perceived the Middle East market as good (and Middle Easterners as not very sophisticated) and, therefore, fertile ground for easy sales. Also, by presenting itself as a pioneer and an expert on Middle East markets, BE could improve its image in Australia. Once BE was established in Iran, other Australian companies were likely to use BE's services, which would help in defraying costs.

Retaining Salesman

BE wanted to make a low-cost entry into Iran, a country that might serve as an introduction to other Middle East markets. James Allen, a young Indian salesman with BE's agent in Bombay who had performed remarkably well in developing the Indian market, emerged as a candidate for developing the Iranian market. McBain decided to retain Allen directly as BE's employee for the following reasons: (1) It would cost far less to send Allen from India than to send someone from Australia or Europe. (2) Allen was likely to better understand the business philosophy and operating practices of the Middle East than would someone from Australia. (3) Allen had already demonstrated his effectiveness in selling by developing the Indian market. (4) Allen was geographically much closer to the Middle East, particularly the Gulf and Iran, and would be able to offer it much better service than would somebody stationed in Australia. (5) Allen hoped to emigrate to Australia, and good performance in the Middle East could encourage BE eventually to offer him a position in Australia. In one of his meetings with Allen, McBain had dangled the prospects of a position in Australia.

Allen was invited to visit BE in Australia. He spent most of his time with McBain, who took him to various job sites and factories. In more than two weeks of constant travel, McBain stressed the great potential that existed in the Middle East, his personal conviction that the markets could be penetrated, and the personal rewards to him and to Allen and anyone else who would associate with the company's efforts in the region. Allen, a young man seeking to make his entry into the international field with a non-Indian company, was a most enthusiastic listener. Having never visited the Middle East, his knowledge was no greater than was McBain's, but both were aware of the large amounts of foreign exchange being earned by these countries. Neither man, however, evaluated carefully the requirements of Middle East markets or the expenditures required of the company in order to achieve realistic sales targets.

In accepting the assignment, Allen thought he was covering all flanks. BE would be paying him to develop expertise on Iran and other Middle Eastern countries. If the market grew, he would be very strongly positioned to dictate fresh terms to BE. If BE was not successful, he would still have acquired valuable field experience in the Middle East which he could then use to gain a position with some other company.

BE retained Allen on the following terms: $7,000 per year, plus $3,000 expenses, plus 3 percent of sales as commission, plus actual expenses incurred in traveling. As an indication of its interest in systematic and long-term development of Middle East markets, BE planned to keep $120,000 worth of equipment and spares in stock in Iran, in order to provide quick delivery and demonstration to local users.

Visit

Allen had never visited Iran or any other Middle Eastern country. He did not have any contacts in the Middle East and did not speak the local languages (Farsi or Arabic), and BE could provide no contacts or backup in Iran other than letters of introduction to the Australian trade commissioners in Iran and the Gulf countries.

The trial arrangement with Astra was on the brink of collapse. Astra charged BE with not providing adequate literature, inventory, technical support, and after-sales technical assistance. Astra also claimed that McBain and Hawkins did not attach sufficient importance to the Middle East, and cited as evidence the small amount of time they spent in Iran and neighboring markets.

BE was not entirely happy with Astra. McBain felt that Astra represented too many foreign companies which were often selling the same product and that, as a result, it was not providing the support necessary to offset the better established European companies, whose products were more readily accepted by local buyers. Therefore, two weeks before Allen was to reach Tehran, BE terminated its understanding with Astra. The president of Astra and other members of the organization lost no time in criticizing BE in local trade and industry circles. Allen was to discover these developments upon his arrival in Tehran.

In order to prepare for his work in Iran, Allen visited Middle Eastern embassies in New Delhi for information and discovered that information on the countries he would be exploring (Iran and the Arab countries of the Gulf) was very limited. Requests sent to the Middle East for information went unanswered. Allen was not entirely sure of the "inner" thinking or planning of BE on the Middle East. He was not happy about the prospects of being away from his family for long durations.

In August, Allen went to Iran and checked into the Intercontinental Hotel in Tehran. He had $2,500 from BE for six weeks of expenses. BE had told Allen of a German named Dietz who had had some dealings with BE in Iran in the past. Dietz, an entrepreneur with a hustler mentality, had left the Iranian office of a Germany company to set up a company of his own. Upon arrival in Tehran, Allen discovered that Dietz was busy with his own work and was not interested in entering into any kind of arrangement with BE. However, Dietz offered Allen space in his office if BE would share the costs of Dietz's office space. Allen concluded that Dietz was not a useful local contact.

To commence his market research, Allen scanned the newspapers, which listed Iranian companies seeking different types of agencies and local representation, visited the various government agencies and embassies for information, and contacted research and consulting organizations. One evening while standing at the bar in his hotel, he struck up a conversation with a Sikh gentleman and explained to him what he was doing in Tehran. The Sikh gentleman said that his brother, a longtime resident of Iran, had just established a new company in the construction business, Pars Construct, and might be interested in talking to Allen.

Pars Construct was a company established by three former employees of Changiz and Company, a leading Iranian construction material supply company which was also the local agent for German manufacturers of cement mixers. Pars

Construct was anxious to exploit the construction boom in Iran. The three partners had expertise in complementary areas. Mr. Mahmudi, formerly sales director of Changiz, became the sales director of Pars Construct with primary responsibility for selling to Iranian customers. He put up the major part of $50,000 required for the initial capitalization of the company. Mr. Shirazi, former financial director of Changiz, had joined an Iranian bank. He was appointed as the financial director of Pars Construct on the assumption that his position with the bank would assist Pars Construct in gaining access to funds to finance the company's business. During the day Shirazi worked with the bank, and during the evening he worked with Pars Construct; it was rumored that he also was involved in other projects. Mr. Singh was the sales manager of the company. Of Indian origin, Singh retained Indian citizenship although he was a longtime resident of Iran. He was fluent in English and Farsi. His knowledge of English made him a valuable addition to the top management team in dealing with foreigners; and it was hoped that over time he would take a greater role in domestic sales as well. Pars Construct felt that it was familiar with the local market, but it felt it had to secure as much foreign representation as it could in order to penetrate the local market effectively.

Allen met with Pars Construct in its impressive office. He was greatly relieved that he could discuss business with somebody like Singh who spoke fluent English. Pars Construct possessed some knowledge of the cement mixer market based on its earlier experience with Changiz. Pars sought an exclusive distributorship from Allen. Allen wanted to test Pars for six months before appointing it as the exclusive agent of BE, and he responded to Pars' request by offering what amounted to an exclusive arrangement but without a legal contract.

Allen was not entirely happy with his selection of Pars but it was the best he could do under the circumstances. All the leading Iranian companies had arrangements with well established international companies, and these would be hard to approach. Many new companies had mushroomed as a result of the Iranian boom, and several such as Pars Construct were offshoots by former key executives of well established local companies. Allen was also aware of McBain's desire to show quick results, and selection of a local distributor was viewed by him as an important first step. Allen was anxious to demonstrate to the Australian management that he could establish BE's position in Iran.

Allen could not investigate Pars Construct for several reasons. It was not listed in any of the directories. Allen had no contacts in the local business community nor did he read or speak Farsi, which severely limited his ability to move freely.

Pars Construct sought an association with BE for several reasons. First, it was interested in making as much money as possible in as short a period as possible, and BE was viewed as a bird in hand. Second, it had no knowledge of technical matters and no personnel who could offer after-sales service. Pars Construct viewed its function as securing orders and handling local procedures, such as customs, while letting the foreign company handle everything else, particularly the after-sales service. BE was promising assistance in these areas. Third, Pars Construct knew that a number of companies were coming to Iran and that the influx would result in a weeding out of local companies. The firm hoped to position itself as one of the better established companies in order to survive this weeding out. BE offered a takeoff point for Pars, especially in seeking additional foreign representations.

Pars had other characteristics that made it particularly attractive for Allen. The company employed an Indian in its senior management, and Allen was more comfortable with such a company than with one whose management was wholly Iranian. Language was not a problem in dealing with the local representative. Singh invited Allen to his home, which made Allen feel less homesick.

In Tehran, Allen made the rounds of the possible buyers to develop a market report for submission to BE. He faced the following problems: (1) He did not read or speak the language, and the information available was in Farsi. (2) On many points, there was simply no information available. (3) Pars Construct was not willing to offer him introductions because it did not have a formal relationship with the Australian company. (4) Allen had no access to those in Tehran who would know of major projects that might use cement mixers. (5) Allen did not have contacts with the major international construction firms that might use his product. (6) He was very short of funds. The $2,500 did not permit him to entertain prospective buyers, which is a major requirement of selling in the Iranian market.

Allen encountered more general problems as well. He had heard a rumor from a local dealer of cement mixers that BE was planning to establish a manufacturing operation in Iran. This caused him considerable embarrassment because he knew nothing of this development, and he lost face with the local dealer, who questioned Allen's importance in the BE organization. Since the changing requirement of the local market demanded constant modification of terms of sale, Allen was obliged to refer almost everything to Australia. These modifications included the understatement of invoices to facilitate custom clearance in Iran, longer payment terms, and use of a bank other than the one preferred by the Australian company. BE was unable to respond quickly because the sales manager in Australia did not understand the reasons for the modifications being proposed by Allen and the local agent. This delay in response to Allen's inquiries seriously hindered his efforts in generating sales.

In six weeks, Allen sold six cement mixers and was convinced that there was a much larger market. He also realized that the local market could be developed only if the company maintained local presence through a representative office and stationed one or two technicians to offer training and after-sales service for the mixers sold.

BE was inclined to establish a local representative. However, facing the problem of generating enough sales to pay for
the cost of a local office, it was not willing to make the initial investment. Allen submitted a rough estimate to McBain
amounting to $126,000 for one year of expenses.

Office space	US$ 20,000
Office equipment and furniture	5,000
Secretary (bilingual)	12,000
Car (purchase price)	10,000
Driver, bilingual (40 hrs/week)	8,000
Apartment rental (three-bedroom to be shared by Allen with BE technicians and executives)	22,000
Local travel (within Iran)	7,000
Office expenses (telephone, cables, etc.)	5,000
Entertainment (promotion)	7,000
Allen's salary (gross)	30,000
	$126,000

Another severe problem for Allen was unavailability of
parts, which resulted in poor service to clients. A vicious
circle plagued Allen—BE wanted Pars Construct to maintain
an inventory of parts, but Pars would not do so because of
its shortage of funds. Allen reminded BE that in its original
discussions, BE had planned to keep equipment and parts
worth $120,000 in Tehran. BE regretted that it could not
proceed because of a shortage of funds. Delays in replacing
machine parts caused frustration and a very poor image for
BE in the local market.

Because some sales had been made, Pars wanted BE to
provide a technician's services for training local users, for re-
pairs, and for assistance in selling, especially where technical
aspects were important. Pars Construct had repeatedly requested a technician, and it was only in response to an ulti-
matum from Pars Construct that BE sent a technician from
Australia. However, the technician fell ill on the way to
Tehran and returned to Australia. Pars Construct's customers

were complaining bitterly and spreading the word of Pars' poor business practices, and Pars in turn was blaming BE. Allen, caught in the middle, was expected to act, but he had neither the money nor the authority to do anything.

BE asked Allen to secure a technician from India who had worked on the BE mixers sold in India. BE figured that a person from India would be cheaper than someone from Australia. However, the need in Iran was urgent and it would be difficult for Allen to find an Indian willing to give up his job and move to Iran for a company that offered him no security and was unable to pay Allen's salary and expenses. (Allen had been with BE for four months and had received only one month's salary.) Nonetheless, Allen started to make inquiries in India.

Bowmar and Wheeler were two technicians employed by BE in Australia. Because BE was experiencing a loss of business and did not want to keep the two on its payroll, it financed their purchase of a cement mixer service operation. Their business prospered initially, but within six months it was losing money. Bowmar and Wheeler were looking for new opportunities at the time that BE faced strong demands from Pars Construct for technicians to service the mixers. McBain convinced them that Iran was a land of opportunity and that their services were in great demand. In order to get them started, he offered them the exclusive after-sales service contract with BE in Iran. He assured the two that they could earn a great deal of money in a short period of time and added that Iran was only one of the booming Middle Eastern markets for mixers and related services.

BE, however, did not wish to incur any expenses for the services of Bowmar and Wheeler, and an arrangement was worked out with Pars Construct whereby it would retain an additional 5 percent commission to pay the salaries and living expenses of the two technicians. Allen recognized that this arrangement would work only if there were sufficient sales.

An additional problem arose between BE and Pars because

the technicians' responsibility was never clearly specified. Bowmar and Wheeler viewed themselves as independent agents available to Pars Construct for work on BE mixers. BE viewed them as informal representatives of BE with freedom to accept other assignments contributory to sales of the BE product. Pars Construct, however, viewed Bowmar and Wheeler as its employees subject to its wishes.

The technicians' effectiveness was severely limited in Iran. They did not know the language and were unable to instruct the workers on how to use the equipment. The manuals were all in English, which further complicated the task of local training. There were no provisions made for transporting the technicians between job sites, and they lost considerable time and money in doing this themselves. There was little social life. The technicians had no knowledge or interest in Iran's culture or history. They felt they were there to do a job and make more money than they could in Australia, and they hoped to return to their families in Australia in about a year.

Pars Construct refused to look after the technicians, because it did not have a formal arrangement with BE; it simply wanted to use BE's services when the need arose. Allen was unable to do much because he faced the same problems as did the technicians. All he could do was to commiserate with them about working for a company that was unable to meet their needs. However, Allen did not wish to return to India and hoped that doing a good job for the Australian company might mean a residence permit for himself and his wife in Australia. The Australian technicians had few alternatives; the Australian construction industry was in a slump, and there were not many opportunities elsewhere they would care to take. The three tried to adjust as best they could to the circumstances.

Meanwhile, the Australian company was undergoing major changes. It was in receivership and therefore severely strapped for funds. The promising Middle Eastern markets required expenditure of resources it was unable to provide. Additionally, top management was too preoccupied with salvaging the Australian situation to give much attention to the requirements of the Middle Eastern market. The sales manager who had dealt with Allen left the company. The managing director became responsible for the Middle East, but all his energies were devoted to sorting out the company's legal problems in Australia. The original $2,500 was exhausted and Allen was continually short of funds. Repeated urgent telegrams resulted in additional funds being sent. Allen had left the Intercontinental Hotel and taken an apartment with Bowmar and Wheeler to reduce costs. Meanwhile, he was desperately trying to maintain some presence in the local market.

By about the first quarter of 1975, the Iranian market underwent a major change. The government halted major projects, tightened credit, imposed major restrictions on credit, and generally went after the land and real estate speculators who had made a great deal of money. These developments dramatically affected BE's business. Pars Construct was unable to sell BE's product. It was sorely lacking in cash, and was simply not prepared to function in an uncertain market.

Allen's situation was desperate. He was short of funds, as BE had paid only one month's salary in the past four months. McBain was highly uncommunicative with Allen, and the prospects for BE in Iran were bleak. Allen faced other problems as well: (1) His efforts to have the literature translated into Farsi and Arabic were unsuccessful, because neither Pars nor BE was prepared to pay for it. (2) The image of the company was tarnished because of poor performance on earlier business. (3) Top management had simply not deemed it important enough to visit the Middle East to gain an understanding of the needs and requirements. Given BE's financial situation, it was unlikely that management would spend the resources to become involved in the Middle East. (4) Pars Construct was threatening to institute a legal suit against

BE for nonperformance of contract terms. (5) The Australian technicians had threatened to resign because they had not been paid, and Pars Construct was creating problems for them by not assisting in gaining clearance from the immigration authorities.

A detailed memorandum from Allen to McBain highlighted these and other problems. McBain was wondering what to do. The Middle East remained an exciting market, and if BE withdrew from Iran, it would be difficult to penetrate the Middle East at a later stage. He concluded that he must first try to answer what had gone wrong and why, and what would be required to correct the situation. He could not help but wonder whether Allen had been a poor choice.

3
Aram Construction Company: Selling Prefabricated Housing in the Middle East

Ashok Kapoor

This case study presents the efforts of a successful entrepreneur in organizing for the sale of "instant accommodation" in the form of prefabricated housing in the Gulf. The difficulties faced by the company can be traced to several causes, including attitude and objectives of senior management and the lack of a systematic approach to developing the appropriate marketing strategy. Some of the issues raised in the case include the following: (1) The company needs to adopt a longer-term perspective instead of a purely short-term orientation, and the time horizon used will determine the approach for establishing a presence in the host country. (2) Operating conditions of the region require the presence in the country of executives with decision-making authority. (3) The company must provide a service or product that, in the eyes of host country decision makers, meets an existing and significant need. (4) The executives being assigned to the region must have prior experience working with each other as a team.

As you read the case, keep the following issues in mind: the reasons for Pieters' lack of success to date in the Gulf, and the specific changes Pieters must make in his operations to improve the chances of success, especially if he should manufacture prefabricated housing units in the Gulf.

*   *   *

André Pieters had been a very successful entrepreneur in Africa. In the 1960s and the early 1970s, he had established sizable real estate development operations in several African countries. Pieters had been astute in developing projects which were then sold to individual investors. However, in early 1970, he confronted growing conflicts with his local partners along with the prospects of potential action by some of the host governments against one or more of Pieters' companies. These developments, coupled with his desire to return to Europe after many years of stay in Africa, convinced Pieters that he should sell his holdings in Africa and return to Europe. He liquidated his assets and realized very handsome profits.

Upon returning to the Netherlands, Pieters acquired one of the leading property developing companies and intended to penetrate the growing European market for housing. His basic objective at this time was to identify and conquer new areas. Europe was a far more mature, regulated, and highly competitive market than Africa. Pieters' early forays into European markets revealed that the volume of financial resources and organizational capacities required were far greater than what he could command.

Determined to explore new business areas, Pieters sought an investment opportunity elsewhere. The markets of the Middle East, greatly lubricated by the recently acquired oil wealth, were a strong magnet for Pieters. He directed his attention to the Middle East and commissioned a report in early 1974 to identify areas and countries where he should consider operations. He did not specify any preference or priorities with respect to countries or industries. His two primary objectives in exploring the Middle East were to make profits in the short term and to reinvest them for developing a longer-term operation in several Middle Eastern countries. Pieters also felt that his experience in Africa could be applied in the Middle East. He had visions of playing a leading role in attracting investments from the Middle East to Africa. Given the wealth of raw materials in Africa and the fact that several African countries had sizable Muslim populations, Pieters felt that the Middle Eastern countries would be interested in investing in Africa.

Pieters was anxious to move as quickly as possible in his Middle East venture, fearing other organizations would beat him to these markets unless he acted quickly.

The report commissioned by Pieters for entering Middle Eastern markets presented the following preliminary observations:

1. Construction would be a major growth industry for several years. The market demand estimates were far in excess of existing accommodations and the volumes anticipated in the development plans of various countries.
2. Pieters should view the Middle East in a long-term context because the Middle Eastern region would continue to possess sizable resources for many years to come.
3. Pieters should focus upon the smaller Arab countries of the lower Gulf prior to penetrating the much larger markets of Saudi Arabia.
4. Pieters and his organization should adopt a low profile and be extremely careful to maintain credibility. Loss of credibility would result in loss of potential business.
5. Pieters should identify specific projects in construction (residential, office, hotels) and establish one of these projects on a pilot basis in order to gain an understanding of the region.
6. An executive with expertise in developing operations in the Middle East should be retained immediately to provide direction. Efforts to develop the market from Europe without the continued presence of responsible leadership within the selected Middle Eastern markets would be ineffective.

7. The major problems which Pieters would face would
   be in implementation of projects and not in identifying areas of demand and profitability.
8. Pieters must identify and carefully study potential
   local partners.
9. Local partners might be selected on the basis of their
   influence and professionalism. Serious conflicts of business philosophy and styles of operations would exist.
   Families whose younger members had been educated
   in the West might be a useful point of reference in
   that younger members were likely to be better informed
   and more willing to adopt a Western business approach.

The report to Pieters concluded by recommending that a
detailed critical path analysis be developed for the specific
pilot project. This would highlight the types of issues that
the organization would encounter, especially with respect to
implementation, and awareness of such issues would allow
the organization to take corrective actions from the very
beginning.

Pieters received the report and concurred with the recommendations presented in it. However, he felt that the additional time expended in discreet inquiries and careful planning
would result in loss of highly attractive and potentially lucrative business opportunities in the Middle East. While he
hoped that the region would provide long-term prospects,
he also wanted short-term benefits. He further argued that
the planning aspects could, in fact, be undertaken while the
organization was being structured in the Middle East.

The Visit

Pieters proceeded to visit several countries in the Gulf and
emerged with a highly positive report on the prospects in the
region. He was convinced of several points. First, the Arabs
and the Iranians were not more sophisticated in business

matters than were the Indians in Africa, and he felt his success in business transactions with the Indians augured well for dealing with Middle Easterners. Second, unlike property development companies from Europe and the United States, he was better positioned to deliver housing and accommodation projects in the Middle East because of the similarities between many African countries and the Middle East. Supervisory personnel and workers would be imported from African countries to complete projects in the Middle East. The social, cultural, and religious factors as well as the problems of living conditions would not prove to be a disincentive for his workers from Africa. In contrast, personnel brought by European and American companies from the developed countries might have greater difficulty adjusting to the Middle East environment. Third, the individuals he had met on his visit to the Middle East were highly enthusiastic and strongly supportive of his quickly entering the region. Fourth, Pieters felt that he had finally found the ideal region for his operations because of its unlimited financial resources, lack of a strong regulatory environment, and limited sophistication in business and technical areas.

Other members of Pieters' organization did not fully agree with his assessment. However, given his enthusiasm and confidence in his project, the other members registered little complaint.

Specific Actions

Pieters recognized several limitations in his organization for operating in the Middle East. First, he did not have a senior executive on the scene. Second, the Middle East interested Pieters for its potential, but it was not a region where he intended to spend much time. Third, he had hardly any contacts in the Middle East. Fourth, none of his executives had any experience in the region.

Pieters also felt that he possessed two strengths in the eyes of Middle Easterners: he had demonstrated his interest in the region by establishing his presence there, and he would be able to offer decisions on proposals much more quickly than would larger companies entering the region. Pieters assumed that the Middle Easterners would place a higher value on securing quick decisions than on the credibility and the reputation of individual executives and companies.

Pieters had determined that his entry into the Middle East should be in the housing sector. Because the number of visitors and permanent residents in the region was multiplying rapidly, the need for housing was critical. Conventional housing would be available only after a period of time, and the immediate need was for some sort of instant housing.

Pieters settled on prefabricated housing as a means of alleviating part of the short-term accommodation shortage. It could be delivered rapidly, assembled very quickly, and contained all the essential features sought by expatriates being assigned to the region. The cost of prefabricated housing on a landed basis would compare favorably with that of a conventional construction. For these reasons, Pieters was confident that prefabricated housing projects would offer handsome profits.

Pieters elected to delay considering the possibility of local manufacturing of prefabricated units because it would take considerable time to locate a desirable partner, to negotiate a project with him, to train personnel, and to create an acceptance of a locally manufactured (instead of an American-made) prefabricated house. American products were deemed superior, especially in the accommodation industry.

Sourcing

The challenge for Pieters was to arrange for a supply of prefabricated units from the United States. Fundamental questions he was faced with included the following: (1) who the manufacturers of prefabricated units are; (2) the extent to which they are currently operating in the Middle East; (3) the extent to which they are willing to make modifications in the product to suit the environmental context of the Middle East; (4) the kinds of financing arrangements sought by the suppliers; (5) the freight configurations for shipment of homes from the United States to the Gulf; (6) the kind of technical assistance provided by U.S. manufacturers for the assembly of units shipped to the Gulf; (7) the price structure likely to be accepted by potential customers in the Gulf; (8) who the potential customers are likely to be; (9) what the preference of the expatriate versus the Arab will be for prefabricated units; (10) what kind of an organization will be needed in the Gulf to sell and provide after sale service of prefabricated units; and (11) who the individual responsible for this particular project should be.

Pieters visited the United States, and after discussing his project with several companies he reached the following general conclusions. First, the U.S. market for prefabricated homes was depressed, which made the manufacturers receptive to any prospect of sales. Second, many companies in this industry were small and financially weak and had no knowledge of international operations. Third, American manufacturers were eager to sell to the Middle East but were ignorant of the particular requirements of that region in terms of product modifications. Fourth, the manufacturers did not have the capability to penetrate Middle Eastern markets on their own. Fifth, there had been visits by individuals from the Middle East to explore the possible sale of prefabricated units in the Middle East, which, however, had produced no specific orders. Several companies had expended considerable time and a few had supplied demonstration units, but none had made any sales. Consequently, a general skepticism existed among the manufacturers concerning prospect of sales in the region.

Pieters felt that he could best realize immediate sales of prefabricated units by contracting for the purchase of American units. His agreement with a U.S. manufacturer specified that the manufacturer would sell exclusively through Pieters in the Middle East, that there would be no minimum volume or dollar amount of sales guaranteed to the manufacturer, that each unit would be supplied to Pieters at 25 percent below list, and that the manufacturer would send a technician to the Gulf for assembly for every four units sold.

Implementation

Pieters' first task was to assign James Morgan, a longtime associate with extensive experience in Africa, to the Gulf. He had remained with Pieters when Pieters shifted his operations to Europe, but his wife and daughter had remained in South Africa.

Morgan was very critical of the prefabricated housing industry. He favored conventional housing and regarded prefabricated units as artificial, cheap, and not worthy of his engineering, design, and construction skills. Morgan had never been to the Middle East. He did not speak the language, had no knowledge of the local customs and, in fact, did not hide his displeasure in being assigned to the Gulf. A rather reserved individual, he made little effort to cultivate friendships with host country nationals. He felt that the sooner the project failed, the earlier he would be reassigned, and he hoped the reassignment would be to South Africa. In accepting the position to the Middle East, Morgan had been led to believe that his primary responsibility was to manage the development and construction of conventional housing of the type he had been responsible for in several African countries. However, upon arrival in the Gulf he discovered that he was increasingly responsible for the prefabricated housing operation.

Pieters also retained two new executives for the Gulf operations. In the course of his discussions with a leading European international bank, he had met a junior executive named James Delaney who shared Pieters' enthusiasm for the Middle

East. Because of the limited prospects for rapid advancement, Delaney wanted to leave the bank to try his fortune in the Middle East. Pieters offered Delaney a position, feeling the projects would need financing and Delaney possessed the necessary banking affiliations. In addition, Delaney was young and enthusiastic and would be more amenable to control by Pieters than an older or more experienced person might be. Delaney was asked to conclude his affairs with the bank; two weeks later he presented himself to Pieters in Europe, who asked him to proceed directly to the Gulf.

The other new executive was Hans Kimm, a German. He was made responsible for securing large government construction projects and for selling prefabricated housing units on a large-scale basis. Kimm was in his early forties and had no experience in the Middle East. He had just left an airplane manufacturer and wanted to try his wings in the Middle East.

The three executives assigned to the Middle East—Morgan, Delaney, Kimm—had never met each other prior to their arrival in the Gulf. They had quite different personalities and different motives for moving to the Gulf. Morgan was a long-time associate and trusted colleague of Pieters but, because of his distaste for the prefabricated housing industry and the region, viewed his assignment as a short-term one. Delaney and Kimm were seeking to explore the potentials in the Middle East without having to invest their own money. They felt that working for Pieters' organization would allow them to do this, but they did not expect to remain with Pieters very long.

Pieters had discussed possible local partners with a number of individuals in Amsterdam. He had sold one of his apartments in Amsterdam to a sheik from the Gulf and asked him for possible introductions to other influential individuals from his region. In the course of explorations on an oil barter arrangement, he was introduced to a Lebanese who recommended his associates in the Gulf as possible partners. Pieters met with one of these associates in Paris and agreed to the following: the associates would receive 5 percent of sales as commission; they would provide land for display of prefabricated units; and over time they would offer introductions to appropriate business contacts in the region.

Because he wanted to move quickly, Pieters did not adequately investigate the background, credibility, and standing of his Lebanese associates in the Gulf. He was relieved to make arrangements for the implementation of his housing project without having to proceed to the Middle East. (Pieters had decided to ignore a comment to him by a European banker in the Gulf that an influential trading family was seriously exploring the feasibility of local manufacturing of prefabricated housing to cater to regional needs.) Shortly after the agreement was concluded, four prefabricated units were sent to the Gulf. Brochures, contracts of sale, and price lists printed in English were circulated. The prefabricated housing park was set up within a month.

About three months after their arrival in the Gulf, Delaney and Kimm decided to leave Pieters. Their decisions were reached independently, but both had found better prospects. They remained in the same town where Pieters' prefabricated unit park was located and complained to other people in the community about what they felt was Pieters' unprofessional conduct. Pieters was now faced with the additional problem of having two of his former executives criticizing him to potential customers. Morgan became the key individual for the prefabricated housing operations after the departure of Delaney and Kimm.

The prefabricated housing park was attracting approximately twenty visitors per week, composed on the average of six Arabs and fourteen non-Arabs. The hostilities in Lebanon had resulted in an influx of Lebanese, all of whom needed accommodations. Customers arriving at the prefabricated housing park were handed literature on the prefabricated units which told the prices of the demonstration units and indicated a delivery requirement of 60 to 90 days.

After six months of operations, Pieters was concerned by the fact that he had spent approximately $750,000 on the project but had not sold one prefabricated unit. Inquiries about the prefabricated units were still being received, and Pieters felt his original assumptions leading to the decision to enter the Middle East were still sound. However, the bottom line was still very much in the red.

Pieters turned to Morgan for his comments on why the prefabricated units were not selling. Morgan was at first reluctant to talk, but later cited the following reasons for lack of performance in the Gulf: (1) the company had engaged in serious marketing mistakes; (2) it did not have sales personnel who could speak Arabic; (3) local social niceties such as serving tea or coffee to potential customers were not followed; (4) no information was provided on the technical aspects of the prefabricated units; (5) no effort was made by the company to modify the units to meet local conditions; (6) the organization did not offer sufficient assistance in the erection of the prefabricated units; and (7) the organization had made no provision for after sales service.

Morgan reminded Pieters that he had never wanted to be in the Middle East and that he had so warned Pieters from the beginning. Pieters had spent little time in the region. He had made several flying trips from Europe for only a few visits of a day or two, and had not developed a knowledge of the region or relationships with key decision makers in order to promote his business. The lack of continued interest and meaningful presence of senior management had a major impact on the morale of the employees in the region.

The Lebanese associates had not been very helpful. The high hopes they had for growth, fueled by discussions with Pieters in Amsterdam and Paris, were not being realized. They felt that Pieters and his organization were purposely hiding things from them in order not to give them their due share.

Other difficulties for the organization also were evident.

Logistical problems had simply not been fully recognized by the company. The berthing and off-loading of ships and the subsequent transportation from dockside to the prefabricated housing park required considerable time and cost. The Americans retained by Pieters and now operating on their own in the Gulf were criticizing Pieters and hurting the company's reputation in the region. The Indians and Pakistanis retained by the organization were finding it difficult to get along with each other. The price of the units was deemed to be too high.

Morgan informed Pieters that the most important cause for the lack of sales was Pieters' failure to become familiar with the region and his unwillingness to spend time in the country.

After returning to Europe, Pieters reviewed the notes on his conversation with Morgan and examined options open to him. One was to consider establishing a local manufacturing facility for prefabricated housing in the Gulf. The extreme shortage of accommodation would lead to a high demand for the prefabricated units, and the host government might provide import protection especially if the appropriate local partners were involved.

4
Automotive Parts, Inc. (Iran): Problems of a Tripartite Venture

Ashok Kapoor

This case presents the efforts of three parties—the Indian and U.S. partners to an existing joint venture in India and an Iranian businessman—to reach agreement on the terms of a tripartite operation in Iran. Each party's approach to the negotiations is influenced by several considerations which severely limit the prospects of a fruitful collaboration, including the following: (1) The parties need to place due weight on logical and economically sound considerations as well as on subjective expectations and personal relationships. (2) A growing range of companies in developing countries that established joint ventures with foreign companies are beginning to set up joint ventures, especially in neighboring countries. (3) The negotiation strength of a party changes as the value assigned by the recipient to the resources it contributes changes. (4) The catalyst in a multiparty project must have credibility with all interested parties.

Considerations influencing the development of the multiparty venture are also present in bilateral ventures; however, they are likely to be particularly accentuated in the former type.

The following issues are important to this case: the objectives of each group and the reasons for their differing approaches to negotiation, and the specific course of action that the U.S. company must undertake to develop a success-

ful multiparty project in Iran. Consider also an agenda for a
final meeting in Iran between the principals. Which subjects
should be included and why, and how should the discussion
be managed?

* * *

An Indian family had entered into several joint ventures with
American and Japanese companies in the automotive industry.
In the mid-1950s and early 1960s, prospects for the Indian
automotive industry were bright because of the government
incentive for developing it. The management of the Indian
joint venture company was entirely in the hands of the Indian
partners, though the U.S. partners had proportional representation on the board of the company. The U.S. company had
recovered in four years its original investment of $100,000
and ever since had realized handsome profits. Because the
U.S. company was preoccupied with the U.S. market and
exploration of Latin American markets (including a joint
venture in Venezuela), it had not kept in close touch with
the Indian partner. The profits were satisfactory and the
biannual visits of the Indian partner did not encourage the
American partner to visit the Indian company regularly to
observe the Indian operation.

International Expansion

The interest of the Indian family in expanding beyond
India became particularly strong in the early 1970s. It felt
that the domestic market for automotive parts would not
grow rapidly, and that the government would impose further
restrictions on the private sector. In addition, the younger
family members were anxious to prove themselves in the
international environment. They selected two strategies for
foreign market expansion: exports to develop familiarity
with foreign markets and joint ventures with the U.S. partners
in third countries.

The Indian partner was particularly enthusiastic about establishing joint ventures with its existing U.S. partners in third countries for several reasons. First, the U.S. and Indian partners could contribute in areas in which they were particularly strong. For example, for Asia and the Middle East, the Indian company could conduct market research and field exploration and develop feasibility studies at a far lower cost than could the U.S. company. In the process of gaining such information, the employees of the Indian joint venture company would develop a better feel for export prospects which would assist exports both by the Indian joint venture as well as by the U.S. partner. The Indian company's understanding of business and government policies for negotiations in the Middle East made it better equipped for handling certain portions of the investment agreement. This would reduce expenditure of executive time by the U.S. company, especially in the initial stages of negotiations. U.S. executives could then be involved in the negotiations as a project approached maturity. Also, the Indian partner could provide trained manpower from the existing Indian joint venture company for establishing projects in third countries in the Middle East and Asia.

The U.S. company would offer technology, foreign exchange, access to its international markets, and the important benefits of the image of a U.S. company in Asia and the Middle East. An Indian company proceeding by itself into Asia and the Middle East would lack credibility.

Given the requirement of joint ventures in almost all Asian and Middle East countries, a local partner would have to be found making a project into a three-party arrangement. The local partner would provide local capital, land, labor, access to local markets, and good will with the host government.

After a manufacturing base was established in a third country, the operation could then take an active role in developing export markets in the region. The U.S. company would benefit by being able to establish operations and gain exports, which would not be possible as quickly without a three-party arrangement. However, the benefits for the Indian company would be particularly important because, without the association of its U.S. partner, it would not be able to expand effectively into the international arena. The local partner would benefit by gaining a local manufacturing venture and the prospects of exports from it to other countries.

This was a general concept developed by Mr. Singh, the senior member of the Indian family. He felt that if he could establish one successful three-party arrangement in a third country with one of his existing U.S. partners, he would be effectively positioned to suggest and make similar arrangements with his other U.S. partners. While Mr. Singh's concept was sound, he recognized that converting the concept into reality would take considerable effort. It is difficult enough for two partners from two countries to get along; the addition of a third partner from yet another country produces an immensely complex situation.

Mr. Singh kept his U.S. partners informed of his general strategy, and they responded favorably. It was, after all, only a general idea, it did not cost them anything and if something developed they could pursue it seriously. The three areas on which Mr. Singh decided to concentrate were the Association of Southeast Asian Nations (ASEAN—Indonesia, Malaysia, Singapore, Thailand, and the Philippines), Turkey and Iran in the Middle East, and Yugoslavia. His decision on specific countries was to be based on the following criteria: (1) The host country should have free currency convertibility, unlike the severely controlled foreign exchange policy of India. A free currency country would permit considerable freedom of action for further international development by the joint venture company. (2) The automotive market of the host country should offer sufficient volume through a few models of automobiles to justify a local automotive parts industry. (3) The host country should be in geographical proximity to India or possess special relationships with India which would facilitate a greater role by the Indian company.

After exploratory surveys in all three areas, Mr. Singh selected Malaysia for Southeast Asia and explored the prospects of a three-party arrangement with his U.S. partner. The latter declined on the grounds that it did not assign high priority to the ASEAN region and had entered into licensing arrangements that would make it difficult to enter into a joint venture. Yugoslavia was also proposed, but the U.S. company concurred with Mr. Singh's suggestion that a more detailed study should be undertaken by the Indian joint venture company at its expense to determine the prospects of establishing three-party manufacturing agreements in Iran. A representative of the Indian family stationed in Iran for export development was asked to undertake detailed market research.

The U.S. company felt that the venture would not cost anything but would provide access to information; that if anything concrete were to take shape, the Indian partner would have to gain the approval of the U.S. partner; and that the U.S. company could control the Indian partner because of the latter's dependence on it for technology.

Nonetheless, several executives of the U.S. company were concerned with the aggressive and expansionist tendencies of the Indian partner. They feared that the sphere of activity being carved out by the Indian partner was likely to constrain moves into the Middle East and Asia by the U.S. company.

The Market Survey and Feasibility Study

Mr. Singh took a strong personal interest in the feasibility study. He contacted an Iranian friend named Farhad, who was thirty years old and had an M.B.A. from a European university. Farhad was in the automotive business with several joint ventures with leading European companies. Farhad's father was a member of the Iranian business elite with close

ties to senior government officials. He belonged to a *dowreh*—
an informal group composed of cabinet members, businessmen, and armed services personnel.

Farhad had expressed general interest in associating with
the three-party concept. However, Mr. Singh wanted to assess
independently the Iranian automotive industry and to evaluate
other prospective partners. He used Farhad's offices as a base
and visited Iran seven times to discuss in detail with businessmen and government officials the foreign investment climate
and the specific developments and plans of the Iranian automobile industry. Some of these visits lasted as long as three
weeks. Well over 100 people were interviewed. Mr. Singh
brought selected senior executives from his Indian operations
to assist him in the field research and also to expose them to
the Iranian context. These executives served as a sounding
board for some of the observations made by Mr. Singh.

The field exploration was undertaken exclusively by executives of the Indian joint venture company under the control
and direction of the Indian partner. Mr. Singh had not objected to the involvement of executives from the U.S. company. However, he had not sought such involvement. In
retrospect, he felt that greater involvement by the U.S.
company with the actual field explorations would have
provided it with a better appreciation of the local market
and also a greater sense of participation in the final set of
recommendations.

The Iranian had not actively participated in the study
except to offer contacts. Farhad's father maintained that a
feasibility study was a waste of time, and told Mr. Singh,
"Stand on any street in Tehran and see all the cars and
trucks. Why do you need a feasibility study? Don't you
trust our word?" Farhad did not share his father's opinion,
but was too deferential to disagree.

Mr. Farhad was interested in the proposed three-party
arrangement for several reasons. First, it offered a faster
means of development at a lower risk than would be the case

in a joint venture. Second, all the work for the development of the feasibility study would be done by the Indian company, after which the Iranian could decide whether or not he wished to participate. Cost to the Iranian—especially in terms of management time, which was his scarcest resource—was negligible. Third, being familiar with the Indian operations, he had a good idea of what the Indian company would be able to provide. He was particularly interested in rapid training for Iranians and having access to skilled Indian personnel for speedy realization of the operation. Fourth, as all his joint ventures were with European companies, the Iranian had limited experience in dealing with U.S. companies. He felt he should gain experience working with U.S. companies, as they would be playing an increasingly important role in Iran. The three-party arrangement seemed to offer him a means of gradually gaining familiarity with a U.S. company. Mr. Singh's twenty years of experience in dealing with the U.S. company would be highly valuable to Farhad. Fifth, the Iranian sought regional expansion in the Middle East and Asia, and felt that association with Mr. Singh would facilitate such expansion.

Other Negotiation

At the time of the preparations for a three-party agreement, the Indian and the U.S. partners were engaged in another negotiation. The Indian partner had proposed that the Indian joint venture be expanded to include additional product lines. The U.S. company was asked to make additional capital contribution. Furthermore, in keeping with the requirements of the Indian government, the foreign equity interest of the foreign partner would in all probability be reduced to 20 percent.

The U.S. company was hesitant about becoming deeply involved in India at the time. The recession in the United States and the problems of the U.S. automotive industry required the full attention of management, and any negotiations for changing the existing arrangements in India would necessitate expenditure of management time.

Another factor contributing to the U.S. company's hesitation was its joint venture in Venezuela, which had proved to be a major financial disaster for the company. Top management was still trying to determine why the Venezuelan operation soured. Mr. Brown, the executive who was the principal supporter for expanding the Indian operation, had been responsible for the Venezuelan operation, and the failure of the Venezuelan operation had greatly reduced his importance and credibility in the U.S. company. He was removed from foreign direct investment decisions and given limited responsibility for export operations. Mr. Brown had developed a good personal relationship with Mr. Singh and was well thought of by the Indian partners. His drastically reduced standing in the U.S. company meant that the Indian company lost a sympathetic ear at the senior levels of management of the U.S. company.

The Indian partner felt that the response of the U.S. partner to the proposed joint venture in Iran would be conditioned by how much it was pushed on the changes in the Indian joint venture. Given its high dependence on the U.S. company for third-country ventures, the Indian company could not afford to overlook the fact that the existing relationship with the U.S. company would condition future arrangements. Farhad was generally aware of the ongoing negotiations between the U.S. and Indian companies on the Indian joint venture.

The Iranian Project: Nature of the Proposal

The proposal based on the feasibility study submitted to Farhad and the top management of the U.S. company by Mr. Singh recommended the following main features:

Products: Initially radiators and gradually extension into related automotive products in the existing product list of the U.S. company.

Equity: Each partner would possess equal equity interest.

Capital contributions: Approximately U.S. $1 million with a debt equity ratio of 3:1, with the Indian company contributing its share of the equity contribution through provision of services such as training, feasibility studies, and supply of selected components which could be offered by the Indian joint venture.

Market area: Initially limited to Iran and eventually to cover the Middle East, with particular focus on the Gulf and other selected markets such as Egypt where Iran might possess special privileges.

Technical management: Initially to be provided by the Indian partner through deputation of personnel based in the Indian joint venture company.

Board representation: To be equally divided among the three owners. At least 60 percent of the shareholders must support a proposal to carry it in the board. The chairman of the board would be a nominee of the Iranian company, chief financial officer would be an American nominee, and the president would be from the Indian company.

Project Development: Phase 1

Mr. Singh felt it was critical for the Iranian to meet with the U.S. executives, and Singh and Farhad proceeded to the United States, where Farhad was exploring several projects. Singh had arranged for them to travel in an executive jet to a midwestern city. Mr. Singh not only wanted to impress the Iranian partner with the importance assigned to him by the U.S. partner, but also wanted to impress the U.S. company with the importance of the Iranian, and felt that the executive jet was a means for doing so. They were met by a limousine at the airport, and an Egyptian national (Mr. Mansour, who was in the international division) escorted them to their suites at the town's leading hotel.

The wife of the vice-president of the international division called Mrs. Singh to arrange to take her and Mrs. Farhad shopping the same day. This message was relayed to Mrs. Farhad, who refused to accompany the other ladies on the shopping trip on the grounds that she had not been "properly invited"; she felt the wife of the vice-president should have had the courtesy to call her directly. The Indian made an excuse to the American that the Iranian had a headache and would stay at the hotel. The Indian and the American returned in the late afternoon and the American called the Iranian from the hotel lobby to inquire about her health. The operator informed the American that the Iranian was out shopping until 6 p.m. The American was confused but rushed home to get ready for a reception organized for that evening at her home to introduce the Indian and Iranian couples to some of the people in the automotive industry.

While the women were shopping, Singh and Farhad met with McGovern, the international vice-president. They discussed the feasibility study and the general terms stated in it. The Iranian expressed concern that the Indian and the American partners who had worked with each other for a long time might collude to control him. The American laughed and assured Farhad that there would be no such attempts. He reminded him that operating in Iran gave Farhad an advantage, since there were means available to nationals for controlling the foreigners. The American tried to laugh away the question, but the Indian wanted to meet it head on. He had informed the Iranian in general terms of his conflict with the American partner on the proposed expansion program in India. Singh replied that working with the Americans for almost twenty years did not necessarily mean that he liked them, and cautioned the Iranian about inferring that the Indian and American partners were united. Singh had resisted attempts by the American company to view the Indian operation as one of its divisions, and the subject had produced strong conflict between the two parties. The Indian operation, according to Singh, was an independent operation, and Singh would insist on a similar arrangement for the proposed Iranian venture. In any case, Mr. Singh would vote independently, in keeping with his best judgment.

Each of the three parties was concerned about collaboration by the other two for control. Mr. Singh was particularly concerned, as he had struggled with some success not to be subservient to the American. His success, however, was in the project based in India, his own country. In Iran, he would have less strength, especially after the project became operational. The Iranian would acquire the know-how and the American would control the technology. The Indian's strength was in taking the initiative to develop the concept and the proposal; however, once the project became operational, his strength would diminish and the American's position would be strengthened because of his control of the technology. Hence, the Indian was anxious that any agreement be worded at the beginning to protect and promote his interests over time.

Though the U.S. company had had a joint venture in India for a long time, its knowledge of the country was limited, and it knew even less of Iran. As a result, it was concerned about losing control in whatever venture was arranged. Once the project was established and operational, the role of the American partner would be reduced. If the American company repeated its experience in India, where it was not involved in management, the Indians and the Iranians would be the principal parties.

The Iranian stated that the chairman of the board should be from the Iranian company. According to Farhad, since the project was to be located in Iran, the Iranian partner should have the most prestigious position. The Indian and the American partners agreed. The American stated that the financial director and the technical director would have to be from the U.S. company. The Indian and the Iranian voiced no objections.

The American maintained as well that the technical assistance agreement and royalty payments would be for the
account of the U.S. company. While the U.S. company in
turn might ask the Indian joint venture company to undertake
most of the work, the contractual relationship would be between the Iranian and the American company. The Indian
objected strongly to this suggestion. He maintained that the
entire concept from the very early stages presupposed involvement of the Indian joint venture company in areas where it
had expertise. Singh's objections also related to the fact that
technical assistance payments made to the U.S. company
would deprive the Indian company of a major means of paying for its part of the equity in the proposed venture. In
addition, the subservience of the Indian company to the
American company would be reinforced by channelling payments through the U.S. firm.

The discussion between the American and the Indian became
heated. When the Iranian volunteered to excuse himself, the
American asked him to stay, adding, "You might as well get
used to this; these are like the quarrels between two lovers."

Other topics discussed included export rights for the joint
venture, size of operation, training program, and the speed
with which government approvals could be secured. All
three parties recognized that they still were far from an
understanding. The Iranian felt that, while the Indian and the
American had worked together for a long time and could
communicate easily, he had difficulty in understanding the
nuances of what they were saying. Occasionally, the Indian
and the American were aware of their cryptic communication, apologized to the Iranian, and elaborated on their
discussion. As they left the meeting room for a tour of the
factory, the Iranian could not help but feel that he was little
more than an observer.

The Reception

Mrs. McGovern was more confused than concerned about

Mrs. Farhad's behavior. She mentioned it to her husband who suggested that she forget it, and they prepared for the reception that evening to which about fifty people had been invited. The Indian and the Iranian couple came together, and were escorted by Mr. Mansour. When Mrs. McGovern inquired about Mrs. Farhad's health, the latter replied that she was "fine and able to look after herself."

The Indian couple knew many of the invited guests from earlier visits and reminisced about old times. The Iranians felt somewhat left out. One of the guests turned to Mrs. Farhad and said that she must be one of the more liberated Middle Eastern women because she was wearing a Western dress. He added: "Don't the Arabs keep their women hidden from the eyes of all male strangers?" The Iranian replied that they were not Arabs but Iranians and that there were many differences between the two.

Another guest started talking about an Iranian student who visited his house recently and complained bitterly about the repressive policies of the Iranian government against freedom of speech. The host intervened and the discussion moved to lighter subjects.

On the way to the hotel that evening, Farhad asked Singh if the Americans wondered whether India had flying carpets. Singh replied facetiously: "Some of them actually believe it." The Iranian realized that he would have a major task of educating the Americans about his country. If the lack of knowledge displayed by some of the guests was typical of executives in the American company, he would have severe difficulties in a business relationship with them.

Personnel Changes in the American Company

Brown had been moved to a less salient position and he finally resigned from the company. He was replaced by Mr. Olden, a young accountant, whose major assignment was to negotiate the proposed joint venture in Iran. He had no international experience, had been to Europe only on holiday for two weeks, and had never visited Iran or the Middle East. Olden was made a board member of the Indian joint venture company. The young man saw this assignment as a major opportunity to prove himself to the company. The Middle East, particularly Iran, was the major growth region, and notable performance by him could lead to rapid promotions. Additionally, he was excited by the challenge of being responsible for a specific project.

He was briefed over lunch by McGovern on the twenty-year history of the Indian joint venture. Olden spent the next week studying the files. Several of the individuals who had been involved with the Indian project were no longer with the company, and he had to rely on the interpretations of others in the organization who had familiarity with the Indian venture. Olden had decided, however, that his main task within the organization was to attempt to fulfill the objectives established by McGovern. His future progress in the company would be directly influenced by the international vice-president.

In a meeting with McGovern, Olden asked why it was necessary to have the Indian partner for the joint venture in Iran. McGovern did not respond directly, but intimated that the project was now Olden's responsibility, and it was up to him to determine the terms and conditions of the involvement of the Indian partner. Because of existing relationships and other issues faced by the company in India, however, Olden was instructed to keep McGovern fully informed of his actions.

The Indian, the Iranian, and McGovern held additional meetings. During the second meeting, McGovern introduced Olden as the executive who would be handling the proposed Iranian project and also presented him to the Indian partner as the new board member from the side of the American company. Shortly after the introduction, McGovern left for other business and encouraged the three to carry on with discussion of the points they had covered the previous day.

The Indian was confused and somewhat offended. Olden was not familiar with the international, Indian, or Iranian business contexts. Singh was not certain what the motive was of the U.S. company in appointing him as the new board member of the Indian company and as the key man for negotiating the Iranian project. The three-party negotiations would be extremely difficult, requiring extreme sensitivities which only an experienced international executive could provide. The Indian also recognized the disparity of rank between himself and the Iranian on the one side and Olden on the other. He wondered if the U.S. company was indicating that it did not attach much importance to the Iranian project and signaling a new and tougher stance on the Indian operation.

Farhad was particularly distressed by the difference of rank between himself and the young accountant. He was the managing director of one of Iran's leading industrial families and he was used to dealing on business projects with peers. In addition, he felt that, at the delicate stage of negotiations when broad policy issues had to be resolved, it was essential that a senior executive of the American company be present. The accountant would not be able to make any decisions and would have to refer back to McGovern, who in turn would have to gain the approval of the board. The Iranian also noted that he might be placed in a weaker negotiation position vis-à-vis the American and the Indian. As the managing director, he would be expected to offer firm commitments on behalf of his company, and failure to do so would be a loss of face for him. Yet the American negotiator would not have to offer commitments. The Indian, he realized, was faced with the same situation. But Singh had the benefit of knowing the American organization very well and therefore being better able to assess the various positions of the American company. Additionally, Farhad knew that Singh had cultivated independent sources of information on the company in trade circles and also through the recently removed executive (Brown), who had been close to the Indian management.

The Iranian recognized all this. But he was particularly concerned about two points: first, McGovern had violated protocol by not retaining an equivalent level of negotiators; second, the negotiations would take much longer than if the principal decision makers were involved. Farhad was most concerned about losing time, given all the other proposals and projects he was developing in Iran.

In a subsequent discussion, the three agreed that the next step should be the drafting of a letter of understanding to encourage all the parties to focus on specifics. Otherwise, they agreed, the negotiations would drag on endlessly. It was agreed that Olden would take the lead through the corporation's counsel in developing a draft. All three would then meet in Tehran to thrash out the details.

The Iranian invited the Indian to his room for drinks and relayed his misgivings about Olden's appointment. Farhad said that he had several other projects pending and that he was not willing to expend too much time on this one. He also noted that he would not participate in the negotiations unless a senior American executive was involved, adding that as long as Olden was the negotiator for the U.S. company, he would designate one of his junior executives as negotiator. The Iranian concluded by saying that he would decide definitely after the Indian and American made up their minds. If he liked what was proposed he would participate; otherwise he would withdraw and the Indian and the American partners were at liberty to seek association with other Iranian companies.

Singh noted that the Iranian was particularly upset because of what he considered to be a loss of prestige. He also realized that, since the Iranian had withdrawn from any active participation and the Americans were placing the project on a slow burner, he would have to push for an agreement. The Indian asked the Iranian to be patient and wait until they all met in Tehran. Early the next morning, the Iranian left for the west coast for a series of business meetings with companies interested in setting up business relationships with him in Iran.

Olden escorted Mr. and Mrs. Farhad to the airport. During the drive to the airport, he hinted that the size and scope of the project should be increased considerably, since the Iranian market offered considerable potential and a larger project would be justified. The Iranian responded that he was not against a larger project provided it could be justified and provided that decisions could be made quickly. Olden had a copy of the Iranian's itinerary in the United States and promised to be in touch with Farhad before he left the United States for Europe and Iran.

In the afternoon, Olden had lunch with Singh. Several procedural matters had to be resolved on the Indian joint venture. Before the discussion moved to these matters, the accountant stated that he was disturbed by the failure of the Indian company to submit periodic reports. A multinational corporation, he stated, must have systematic reports on prescribed forms from each of its operations in order to control operations effectively. He had decided, therefore, that henceforth the Indian company was to submit detailed and periodic reports on prescribed forms, and he had instructed his secretary to mail a supply of forms to India. He would be happy to explain any of the terms in these forms to Mr. Singh or his Indian staff if the terms were not known to them.

The Indian reacted adversely to the new reporting requirements and to Olden's approach. He stated that the Indian company was not a part of the American company, that it was a separate, independent and self-contained entity, and that he would not agree to submitting periodic reports. He also stated that it was important that the two of them understand each other, as they would be on the board of the Indian company and would be interacting on the Iranian venture. Singh asserted, "It has taken the hard work of two generations of my family to develop my company, and I simply will not accept having it treated as subservient." The conversation shifted to the proposed expansion of the Indian company.

The accountant stated that he was not sure if the expansion was a good idea, and wondered whether or not the Indian company would have sufficient management, especially in view of its aggressive expansion programs in other industries and overseas. The Indian replied that given the past twenty years of efficient management, they were confident of a successful operation. Other factors had to be considered as well. For example, the "emergency" announced by Mrs. Gandhi would have the immediate effect of reducing the Indian market, especially as the "black (undisclosed) money" market was curbed. The recession in India, which had reduced the demand for automotive products (and therefore the need for expansion), strengthened the position of the Indian company in dealing with the U.S. company. However, both Olden and the Indian realized that the decision would be made not on this visit but in subsequent discussions between Singh and McGovern. The Indian informed Olden that he was having dinner with the chairman of the company and would hear his reactions to the Indian and proposed Iranian operations.

The discussion moved on to the proposed joint venture in Iran. Olden felt the Iranian was too preoccupied with other projects to devote much attention to this venture particularly since he flew to the west coast instead of continuing discussions with Olden and Singh. When Olden asked if Singh would consider a larger project, the Indian replied that he was not in favor of a larger venture at this stage, and that it was important not to raise the expectations of anybody, especially the Iranian, unless a larger project was certain. A smaller project, according to Singh, would allow the three partners to work out their own relationships while gaining an understanding of the market. If the smaller project developed smoothly, a larger venture could be considered later.

In subsequent meetings nothing significant was resolved by Olden and Singh. The Indian agreed to get more details on Indian government requirements for the expansion program, and Olden was to develop additional information on the Iranian project. Singh was convinced that the Americans would not expand the size of the project in Iran.

Project Development: Phase 2

Three months after the discussions in the United States, the American, the Indian, and the Iranian met again in Tehran. Farhad did not participate in the discussions but appointed Ahmedi, one of his trusted junior executives, as negotiator. Olden came with the company's legal counsel. Singh was accompanied by the technical director of the Indian joint venture company. The Indians arrived two days ahead of the Americans and held preliminary discussions with Farhad, who maintained the position he had outlined in the United States. He further stressed that he would not be interested in the project if it took more than a month for the Indian and American to reach agreement. The Iranian noted that one of his cousins was then in Japan and had been approached by a Japanese company for a joint venture in Iran. He did not wish to withdraw from the negotiations but he wanted his terms of continued involvement to be clearly understood.

Olden and the counsel arrived in Tehran from New York late in the evening and met with the Indians and Ahmedi over cocktails in the lounge. He gave the draft agreement to the Indians and a copy to Ahmedi, and a meeting was scheduled for the following morning at 9 a.m. to discuss the draft and negotiate the specific points.

The draft contained the following general provisions: (1) Project size was raised to $3 million and each party was asked to contribute up to 25 percent of its equity interest in cash. (2) Two additional products would be included in the project. (3) The chairman of the board would be a nominee of the Iranian partner. (4) The Indian partner was expected to vote along with the American partner.

At the meeting in the morning, the Indian reacted adversely to the proposed agreement. He objected that he could not put up any cash in foreign exchange because of the restrictions of the Indian government; that, given the increase in size of the project, he could not secure the ownership percentage agreed to originally; that the much larger scope of the project was a mistake because a smaller venture would better reveal the teething problem of establishing a project in Iran; and that he would not agree to the requirement of voting along with the American partner.

While the Iranian representative voiced no objections to the proposed terms, he stressed that the Indian and American partners must reach a clear understanding if they were to launch an effective three-party project in Iran. The Iranian did not want the Indians and the Americans to use the Iranian project as a battleground for settling their differences over their project in India. He reiterated that his principals would continue to be interested in the project if it could be finally resolved within thirty days.

Olden reacted sharply to Singh's protestations, and suggested that the Indian should not attempt to "swim in waters which were too deep for him." If Singh could not participate as an equal partner in the project, asserted Olden, then he should settle for a lower equity interest of, for example, 10 percent. With respect to the voting arrangement, Olden noted that as the investment in Iran would be by the Indian joint venture company and not by the Indian partner in the joint venture, and as the Americans were equal partners in the joint venture in India, it was reasonable for them to seek an arrangement for voting similarly. Olden assured Singh that the Americans would seek the full advice and assistance of the Indians in making decisions. Singh interrupted to note that the voting requirement was a breaking point for him. The meeting was adjourned and the three representatives left to consider privately the implications of the developments of that morning.

The Indian and the Americans met in the lobby of the hotel to discuss further their differences. Olden suggested they use his room but Singh refused. The Indian began by saying: "What kind of game are you trying to play?" The Americans responded that they were trying to develop a sound project and to protect their interests. The Indian disagreed sharply, maintaining that Olden was scuttling the project and that he simply did not understand the nature and requirements of doing business in Asia and the Middle East. The U.S. company was going back on its earlier agreement on the size and scope of the project, Singh added, and was trying to squeeze out the Indian company. Singh warned that Olden would not be able to promote and implement the project without the involvement of the Indian partner. The legal counsel was angered at Singh's comments and noted that he was not sure the American company needed the Indian partner in Iran. The Indian rejoined by saying that the accountant would not last long with the American company if his current attitude persisted, and that Singh, as an equity holder, would outlast him in his relationship with the American company. The Indian added: "If you can kick me in the shins in Iran, I will kick you in the stomach in India." Both Singh and Olden realized their discussions had deteriorated to personal attacks upon each other.

On Thursday, Singh left for a brief vacation to the Caspian Sea, planning to return to Tehran on Saturday morning to resume negotiations. Olden and the counsel decided to extend their stay in Tehran.

Olden realized that the Indian might well withdraw from the Iranian venture, and was concerned by the implication of a withdrawal for the existing joint venture in India and for the reaction of the Iranian partner. He decided to meet with another Iranian company that was also in the automotive business. Amouzegar, the founder's son, had been in college with Olden in the midwest. After reminiscing about old times, Olden shifted the conversation to current negotiations with the Indian and the Iranian companies for a three-party arrangement, and described the problems he was having with the Indian company.

Amouzegar asked what the value would be of the Indian company in the project. Olden replied that, while he felt the Indians were not needed, the senior management of the company wanted their participation. Amouzegar noted that his company was planning to manufacture automotive parts in Iran and suggested that perhaps his company might replace the Indian partner. Under such an arrangement, two of the partners would be Iranian and the third partner would be American. Amouzegar stressed that a decision by the U.S. company was urgent, as he was considering other arrangements as well.

Olden said he would check with his headquarters. The office would be closed until Monday and he did not feel that he should call McGovern at home on this matter. Anyway, he would give it thought and talk to him later.

The meeting between Singh, Farhad, and Olden resumed on Saturday morning at 10 a.m. in Farhad's office. Farhad asked if Singh and Olden had been able to resolve their differences. The Indian noted that there were still important issues to be negotiated, which would require that senior management from the American company negotiate directly with their Indian and Iranian counterparts. The Iranian asked Singh if he had had discussions with any other Iranian company for a similar venture. The Indian said, "No."

Farhad then turned to Olden and asked if he had had any discussions with another Iranian company. When Olden replied he had not, Farhad stated with some anger, having learned of the discussion with Amouzegar, that perhaps Olden's memory was failing him. After hesitating, Olden summarized his conversation with his Iranian friend and noted that it was nothing more than conversation and that he had offered no reaction or encouragement to his Iranian friend. Farhad was not convinced but decided not to pursue the matter at the time.

Singh volunteered that if the Americans wished to have him withdraw from the project he would do so. He was having second thoughts about the project, not because of its essential features, but because of the refusal of the American company to assign senior executives to negotiate the project.

The three parties summarized their respective positions. The Indian recommended returning to the original terms. The American advocated some modification of the revised terms but not a total retreat to the original terms. The Iranian stressed that a final decision must be made in three weeks.

5
Arab Potash Company: Project Development

Ibrahim F. I. Shihata

This case describes efforts to establish an inter-Arab joint venture involving the participation of public international organizations and international companies. Several characteristics of such ventures are highlighted.

The Arab Potash Company (APC) is the first multilateral Arab economic venture ever to be conceived and, until 1974, the only such venture to be realized among Arab governments in the industrial field. The agreement establishing APC was prepared under the auspices of the League of Arab States. This regional organization later acted, with little success, as the sponsor of many other multilateral economic ventures. Its sponsorship of the project in its early stages had an effect on some of the later developments.

The founding partners in this venture included six Arab states and one private commercial bank. In a later develop-

Dr. Ibrahim F. I. Shihata is at present the Director-General of the Organization of Petroleum Exporting Countries Special Fund. At the time of writing this case, Dr. Shihata was senior legal advisor of the Kuwait Fund for Arab Economic Development. The case study was part of a larger report by Dr. Shihata to the UNCTAD secretariat and was distributed on October 21, 1975 as UN Document TD/B/AC. 19/R.5.

The views expressed are those of the author and do not necessarily reflect those of the UNCTAD secretariat or the OPEC Fund. The terminology is that of the author. The designations employed and the presentation of the material in this document do not imply the expression of any opinion whatsoever on the part of the secretariat concerning the legal status of any country, territory, city or areas or of its authorities, or concerning the delimitation of its frontiers or boundaries.

ment, majority participation was vested in private investors of different Arab nationalities, thus turning APC from a public international enterprise into a mixed economy joint venture.

Western technology was sought in the implementation of the venture through several consulting, management, and sales agreements. Equity participation of Western partners was also sought and almost realized at one point. It may still materialize in the eventual implementation of the investment. International as well as foreign national lending agencies have been heavily involved in the several attempts actually to implement the project.

Although APC failed for a long time to realize the initial expectation, its experience in arranging the complicated technical and financial details may serve as a useful example for future action in this and other ventures.

It is important to consider the following questions in reading the case: (1) What have been the implicit and explicit issues of negotiation between the shareholders of APC and the management of APC and international companies whose affiliation with the project has been sought? (2) In what ways and why have the issues of negotiation changed over time for the host country (Jordan), the Arab shareholders, public international agencies, and private international companies? (3) What are the requirements for acting as a catalyst in effectively promoting a project such as APC? (4) What are the essential conditions for establishing successful multiparty projects such as APC? (5) What role should the international company play in such ventures?

*   *   *

Interest in the exploitation of the mineral resources of the Dead Sea was initiated by the government of Jordan in the early 1950s. As a first step, the government entered into agreement with an American concern, Chemical Construction Corporation of New York, for the study of the feasibility of establishing a potash plant on the north shore of the Dead

Sea in the old site of the Palestine Potash Company. The study submitted in 1954 recommended the implementation of a project for the production of 70,000 tons of potash per year if positive results were yielded by a pilot plant recommended by the study. A number of Dutch experts were also consulted at that time on the technical aspects of the civil works of the project.

On the basis of these studies the government of Jordan sought the participation of other Arab countries in the financing of the project. The matter was discussed in the Economic Council of the League of Arab States, which approved in January 1956 a draft agreement establishing the Arab Potash Company Limited. On June 21, 1956, this agreement was signed by Jordan, Saudi Arabia, Iraq, Egypt, Syria, and Lebanon, as well as by the Arab Bank, a Jordanian private commercial bank. APC's authorized capital was fixed at Jordanian dinars (JD) 4.5 million (then equivalent to $12.6 million), of which JD 1 million was initially subscribed as founders' shares. A subsequent issue of shares in 1961-62 was subscribed by Kuwait, Qatar, and a number of private investors of different Arab nationalities, whose participation exceeded that of the member governments. As a result, the subscribed and paid-up share capital amounted to about JD 3.2 million, distributed as follows:

Governments	Value JD	
Jordan	500,000	
Iraq	125,000	
Kuwait	125,000	
Saudi Arabia	125,000	
Egypt	125,000	
Lebanon	62,500	
Syria	62,500	
Qatar	50,000	
	1,175,000	
Private	2,029,000	(paid 2,016,011)
Unsubscribed	1,296,000	
Total	4,500,000	

The agreement establishing the company provided that APC's shares, which remained unsubscribed after the public call to subscription, would be covered by the then projected Inter-Arab Financial Corporation. In the event this latter corporation was not established (as was indeed the case), subscription would be made by the founder governments "according to the percentage of their contribution to the budget of the Arab League." This strange requirement has been ignored, however.

Although the agreement did not specify the nationality of the company, it was clear that the corporation would be established as a Jordanian shareholding company to be registered in Amman. No special privileges or immunities were conferred on the company by virtue of its constituent agreement except for its reference to a concession for the exploitation of the Dead Sea minerals, which the company was to acquire by agreement, subject to ratification by law, with the Jordan government. This concession was later granted for 100 years as of February 18, 1958.

The first board of the company was to consist of a representative of each participating government unless its subscription reached JD .5 million or more, in which case it was entitled to two representatives on the board. Representatives of private shareholders were also to be included on the board in a number proportionate to their participation in the subscribed capital. After the large subscription by private investors in 1962 was completed, APC's Articles of Association were amended to provide for the composition of the board of seven members, two to be nominated by the government of Jordan and the rest to be elected by the private shareholders, thus leaving all other Arab governments without representation in the board. This amendment, which was obviously made without the approval of the other participating governments, was justified at the time by the fact that such governments were previously represented by their ambassadors to Amman, who contributed little to the board's activities. The

amended articles provided, however, that an Arab government may be represented on the board only when it subscribed at least JD 250,000 in the company's capital—a
requirement that has not been met by any member government other than Jordan. The amendment has thus emphasized
both the private and the domestic character of the company
and has led, in fact, to lessening the role of other Arab states
in the developments related to the project.

Characteristics of the Venture

From its inception, APC has commissioned a number of
feasibility studies, operated a small pilot plant on the Dead
Sea, and made numerous contacts with various foreign
agencies and industrial companies regarding the financing of
the project. In 1961 Western Knapp Engineering Company of
Los Angeles was commissioned as consultant, and in 1962 it
completed a comprehensive feasibility report for a 250,000-
tons-per-year (tpy) plant, initially projected at an estimated
cost of $36 million excluding the road to the port of Aqaba.
(The plant was originally envisaged to have a 70,000-tpy
capacity.) The Knapp report was the basis for applications
for financial assistance submitted in 1962 by the government
of Jordan to International Development Association and the
U.S. Agency for International Development (AID), and was
to be used in discussions with potential foreign partners.
However, a project based on that report was found unattrac-
tive to potential financiers. At the World Bank's request, a
new feasibility study was completed by Knapp in July 1964.
The revised total cost estimate for the plant was increased to
$45 million, which rendered it economically unfeasible for
the project to produce only 250,000 tons annually. Discussions with potential foreign partners, the most serious with
Dow Chemical, produced no firm agreement or commitment
to invest. Meanwhile an offer made in 1963 by Arthur Mekky
Corporation (the parent of Knapp) to implement the project

and provide management and sales services to it could not be accepted by APC and the Jordanian government.

U.S. AID's continued interest in the project led it, with the World Bank's and APC's concurrence, to entrust Jacobs Engineering Company of California with the reappraisal of Knapp's proposals. The Jacobs report submitted in March 1965 was considered by both the bank and AID to provide a more sound basis for project implementation, although it recommended a plant of twice the capacity envisaged by Knapp. The report concluded that a project to produce initially 500,000 tons of potash was feasible at an estimated capital cost of $60 million, provided that first-class management and marketing could be made available and that financing on appropriate terms was arranged. On the basis of that report, the World Bank gave its approval in principle of a loan of $30 million for the project. Shortly afterwards, AID approved a commitment of $15 million. It was assumed by both agencies that the remaining $15 million would be met by APC's equity after doubling it, and by the inclusion of a foreign partner who would also assume responsibility for the management and operation of the project and provide appropriate assurances for marketing the output, primarily outside the Arab region. It was also assumed that the government of Jordan, which was acting throughout as the sole sponsor and guarantor of the project, would meet the cost of a suitable road to Aqaba and a township on the site and would assume any additional finance in case of cost overruns. The Kuwait Fund for Arab Economic Development, whose interest in the project was sought in late 1965 by the Jordanian government and the World Bank, offered its good offices in interesting private Arab investors to participate in APC's equity.

Subsequently, the World Bank took an active role in the selection of the foreign partner in APC. Discussions held with ten interested multinational companies resulted in the selection of International Minerals and Chemicals (IMC) of

Skokie, Illinois, then accounting for about 30 percent of U.S. and Canadian potash capacity. Negotiations between APC and IMC started in the fall of 1965 and led to the signature of a Memorandum of Understanding in December 1965, which was to be followed by more detailed agreements. According to the memorandum, IMC was to participate in the equity capital of APC by taking 50 percent of the shares after recapitalization of the company at $15 million (not including $2 million of past expenses on the pilot plant and the Knapp report, which, it was agreed, would be written off). IMC was also to have full control over the management of APC and the marketing of its products.

Later in 1966, IMC withdrew its offer, due in part to the rejection by the Jordan government of IMC's proposal to enter into another contract with the Jordan Phosphate Mines Company for the sale of phosphates. Other reasons for the withdrawal were (1) the failure of IMC to break the hold of the Franco-German cartel for the sale of potash in Europe and (2) IMC's fears of an oversupply of potash in the 1970s. As a result, APC had to look again for a new foreign partner. With the assistance of International Finance Corporation, who learned of the project through the World Bank, many multinational companies were contacted. Of these, four showed interest, especially W. R. Grace & Co. Meanwhile, Jacobs and its subconsultants for civil works, Alexandre Gibbs of London, continued technical work on the project. Some of the companies contacted for equity participation raised from the outset the possibility of planning for a plant capacity of one million tons, and Jacobs was asked to study the economies that such a capacity would be likely to achieve.

Results of the Jacobs reappraisal confirmed the soundness of a project with an increased capacity of 1,000,000 tpy. Capital requirements would be $100 million. Renewed discussion among potential financiers (World Bank, IFC, AID, and Kuwait Fund) resulted in a common understanding on a new financial plan, whereby 25 percent of the newly esti-

mated cost would be met by equity and 75 percent by debt
to be provided in equal amounts by the World Bank, AID,
and the Kuwait Fund. The $25 million equity was also to
be covered on the basis of 51 percent by Arab shareholders
(APC), 14 percent by IFC, and 35 percent by a foreign partner to be entrusted with management and marketing. In a
January 1967 meeting of these financing agencies—the
government of Jordan, APC, and W. R. Grace and Company—
it was agreed that a new corporation, to be called Jordan
Arab Potash (JAP), would be formed by APC under the laws
of Jordan to carry out the project. APC would thus continue
in existence holding only 51 percent of the capital stock and
junior subordinated debt of JAP, and would transfer to JAP
the concession agreement to the extent necessary for the
operation of the project. The rest of JAP's equity would be
held by IFC (14 percent) and by a joint company to be
formed by Grace and a partner (35 percent). The government
of Jordan would have a representation in the board of JAP
along with the three shareholders. The joint company (Grace
and its partner) would also enter with JAP into a management and operating agreement as well as an exclusive marketing agreement. The originally envisaged inter-Arab joint
venture was thus to be turned into a Jordanian/American
venture with very little trace of joint Arab action. Details of
these arrangements were later negotiated, leading to the
preparation of a draft new concession law, draft management, and marketing agreements, draft loan agreements between each of the lending agencies and JAP, and draft guarantee agreements between them and the Jordanian government.
The meticulous efforts involved in the process proved, however, to be futile. The final negotiations held in Washington
in early June 1967 were terminated on June 3 at the request
of W. R. Grace because of political developments then prevailing in the Middle East. Two days later war erupted. One
of the minor and less known effects of the Arab-Israeli war
was the shelving of the potash project for many years to come.

Shortly after the war subsided, the World Bank proposed a new "emergency plan" for the project, whereby financing and execution would initially be limited to a pilot program, including studies and trial tests, leaving further steps for discussion in light of the results of this preliminary phase. It was estimated that the pilot program would cost $6 million and last for eighteen months. JAP would still be formed, but with a much smaller capitalization. The government of Jordan and APC would each contribute $1.25 million, with APC being required to put up only $250,000, as the rest of its contribution was to be accepted in kind (the estimated value of the previous studies financed by it). Complementary financing would be met through loans from the World Bank ($1.5 million) and the United States government ($3 million). Although this plan was approved by the Jordan cabinet in April 1968, and a new American concern, Tenneco, was being considered as a potential replacement for W. R. Grace, no action was followed in either direction.

In June 1969, the government of Jordan requested APC to return to its private shareholders the nominal value of their shares up to a maximum of 200 shares per shareholder. This step was complemented in March 1972 by APC's decision to return the nominal value of the shares to the remaining private shareholder, thus reducing drastically APC's subscribed capital. The authorized capital remained unchanged, however.

The Arab governments that had remained "sleeping partners" in APC since their exclusion from its board of directors in 1962 came to express new interest in the project late in 1973. On the recommendation of the government of Iraq, APC convened a meeting of representatives of these governments to discuss with its board members ways of resurrecting the potash project. The meeting, in which each side was blamed for ignoring the other during past developments, recommended that APC apply to the Arab Fund for Economic and Social Development, a regional inter-Arab organization in operation since 1972, for help in the financing of the project.

It also requested APC to resort to the financially able Arab
governments to increase their equity participation in APC
and to contact the governments of potash-consuming countries and interested foreign companies to determine their
participation in its activities. The representatives of the Arab
governments comprised a group of shareholders not represented in the board of the company but holding majority
participation. As such, their legal authority was questionable.
Nonetheless, their recommendations were officially adopted
by APC's board. An application for financing was presented
to the Arab Fund in 1973 and contacts were renewed in the
same year with both the Kuwait Fund and the World Bank.
Jacobs was also asked to look into the possibility of updating
its study of the feasibility of the project.

Late in 1974 APC started a new phase of the project by
the preparation of up-to-date feasibility studies and the construction of a trial dam and dikes in the Dead Sea to help in
the technical evaluation of the project. This phase was estimated to cost $10 million. U.S. AID provided a loan for this
purpose for $6 million, and the World Bank $1 million, while
the remaining $3 million was met by the government of
Jordan. The financing of the actual implementation of the
project was to be discussed with the World Bank, AID, and
Arab sources of the development finance in light of the
results of this preliminary phase.

The pilot project was carried out during 1976 and 1977
with the assistance of consultants Jacobs and Alexandre Gibb.
Based on the results of the pilot project, a preliminary feasibility report was issued by the consultants in 1976, and a
final report in 1978 indicated that a full-scale project for the
production of one million to two million tons of potash was
viable.

The project, as currently envisaged, will be owned and
operated by APC, which is now owned 51 percent by the
Jordanian government, 25 percent by the Arab Mining Company (itself owned principally by four Arab governments),

possibly 10 percent each by the Arab Investment Company (an intergovernmental Arab venture) and the Islamic Development Bank, and the remaining 4 percent by various Arab governments and private investors. APC's shareholders will contribute $170 million equivalent in equity, representing 40 percent of the estimated total project financing requirements of $422 million. The government of Jordan has invited concessionary financing proposals from a number of multilateral, bilateral, and regional financing institutions, including the World Bank, U.S.-AID, the Kuwait Fund for Arab Economic Development, the Arab Fund for Economic and Social Development, and the OPEC Special Fund. These institutions have all given their agreement, at least in principle, to provide a share of the long-term debt financing required. This new financial plan is now expected to be finalized before the end of 1978.

Evaluation

Despite the subscription of a number of governments and private investors of different Arab countries to APC's capital, APC has acted and has been treated as a national Jordanian company. Member Arab governments were initially represented in APC's board, but have since 1962 been practically isolated from the company's activities and have acted as sleeping partners. The company's management and personnel have also been exclusively Jordanian. As a result, it is difficult to evaluate APC, the oldest inter-Arab company, as a joint Arab venture. The participation of different Arab governments in the company's capital may have provided an additional incentive for the different lending agencies which showed interest in financing its activities. Other than this, however, the company has been operating as a local company subject to the strict supervision of the government of Jordan.

The role of the government in this instance was certainly greater than its role vis-à-vis other private shareholding companies. This may have been due in part to the multi-national nature of APC's capital composition, but it can more plausibly be traced to other factors. For a long time the company became a symbol of failure (especially when compared to another potash project implemented by Israel on the other side of the Dead Sea), and has since become an issue in internal Jordanian politics. The keen interest of the government in APC's future has benefited the company to the extent that the former was prepared to provide alone all the financial guarantees required by foreign lenders and to finance the required infrastructure, despite the fact that it was only a minority shareholder in a joint venture.

The difficulties met by APC may be attributed to many factors. The company was formed before the technical and economic feasibility of the project was established beyond doubt. Originally conceived to produce 70,000 tons of potash, APC was soon advised to plan for a production capacity of 250,000 tons, then 500,000, and finally 1,200,000. The "initial" stage for completion of studies and trial tests was undertaken only after more than twenty years of development, while the size of the project and its financial needs remained uncertain. APC management has, on the other hand, played a minor role in its affairs, which were taken up on the whole by the government of Jordan, a minority shareholder. An important major force (the Arab-Israeli War) also hindered implementation of the project in 1967. None of these difficulties could be blamed, however, on the inter-Arab nature of the venture. On the contrary, if other Arab partners had played a more active role in the venture, especially for meeting additional financial requirements, some of these difficulties could perhaps have been avoided, as the most recent developments have amply proved.

6

Color Plant, Inc.: Training Foreign Nationals in the United States

Gary E. Lloyd

This case describes the experience of an American company training host-country nationals in the United States. While both the U.S. company and the trainees have similar objectives, they encounter difficulties in dealing with each other because of their different values, attitudes, achievement motives, educational backgrounds, and criteria of success. Major policy issues faced by both the host country and the U.S. company include the following: (1) In what ways can the transfer of technology be facilitated? (2) What are the determinants of human resource development, especially for large-scale projects being established and made fully operational within a short period of time? The considerations raised in this case are also relevant for the efforts of companies in human resource development within the host countries.

Consider the following questions as you read this case:

1. Assuming that the trainees were Algerian nationals, what cultural attitudes, values, and assumptions would they have similar to those likely to be found in the American company's rural plants in the United States?

2. Imagine that you are an international human resource development specialist called in to design and develop a three-month training and development program for the remaining forty-six middle- and lower-level managers. Assuming that the

trainees are Saudi nationals, on what technical, human, and conceptual skill development would you focus your training and development program, and why? What training methods and techniques would you apply, and why? What changes would be objectives of your three-month training program?

3. You have been invited into the morning meeting described later in this chapter as an international organization development specialist to observe the problems and attitudes of the U.S. managers toward the forty-six trainees. Over lunch the American managing director of the joint venture asks you to conduct the afternoon problem-solving session. He has expressed considerable concern that the type of organization to evolve in the host country be closer to the U.S. company in management philosophy, principles, and performance criteria. Assuming that the forty-six trainees are Iranian nationals, develop an agenda for the afternoon meeting which will solve the managing director's concerns. How would you conduct this meeting? What matters have to be solved before a three-month plan of action can be developed? What human resource development plan would you propose for the next two years? What should be the criteria for determining when the Iranian nationals will take over the managerial jobs of the Americans and third-country nationals?

4. Identify the major determinants of effective transfer of technology which were not adequately recognized by Color Plant, Inc.

*   *   *

In 1975, members of a key merchant family from a prominent electronics manufacturing company in the Middle East approached Color Plant, Inc., a major electronics manufacturer in the U.S., to establish a plant for color television manufacturing in their country. After extensive negotiation over a period of approximately 18 months, the two companies signed an agreement for approximately $500 million to enter into a joint venture operation, with 40 percent owned by the U.S. company and 60 percent by the Middle Eastern company. The U.S. company was to provide the state-of-the-art technology, which included plant and equipment, training and development, and the initial management. The project was to be turned over to the host country nationals as an operating unit in five years.

After receiving the host government's approval, the U.S. company entered the plant implementation phase by selecting an international construction company to perform the plant construction in country under its specifications and under the supervision of the U.S. television manufacturer. The plant under construction was to be a totally integrated state-of-the-art color television plant. Site selection was made and ground was broken in the summer of 1976. The plant was to be on stream and operating within approximately three years, in the summer of 1979.

In the spring of 1977, the U.S. company was to begin the training of local nationals, who represented the source of middle- and lower-level manpower for the plant. About fifty American managers and third-country nationals would staff the upper and middle management positions, gradually turning over these positions to nationals who had performed effectively in the plant and who had potential for further growth in the joint venture. This group was to be selected from 200 middle- and lower-level managers to be recruited, selected, trained, and developed by the U.S. joint venture partner.

From the outset, the U.S. managing director on site insisted that effective human resource development planning be conducted, and that every effort be made to provide opportunity for U.S., national, and third-country nationals to adjust successfully to the work in order to realize the joint venture's objectives. As a consequence, the advance international personnel planners established systems to recruit, select, train, and develop personnel effectively at all levels of the organization. First priority was to recruit, select, train, and develop four groups of fifty potential middle and lower managers to staff the five departments needed to operate the plant. In four six-month training cycles, fifty potential managers were recruited and selected to join the joint venture.

Trainees and U.S. Training

Initially, the fifty trainees were recruited and selected by the national joint venture partner, using a multiple interview format in which the last interview was conducted by an international personnel representative of the U.S. joint venture partner. Final selection of a candidate was the decision of the American partner. All candidates chosen had electrical engineering degrees and English language proficiency and all were between twenty-six and thirty-five years of age. Half of the trainees had degrees from British, ten from American, and fifteen from local universities. Because urban areas and government service were commonly preferred by most individuals in this country, interviewers had difficulty finding candidates who would agree to live in a small town and who were motivated to work with a high-technology private company.

In the spring of 1977, the fifty trainees flew to the United States to start their systems training and development period, arriving first at corporate headquarters for a brief period of general company orientation. They were subsequently assigned to five different plant sites throughout the United States, two of which were in urban areas and three in rural areas.

At each location, there was a personnel/training coordinator responsible for receiving, paying, and coordinating the activities of the trainees during their stay in the United States. The plant coordinator was to interview the trainee and determine, based upon his background, experience, and education, what his training needs were and how his skills could contribute toward the company's needs in the new venture.

Skilled in both personnel and training, the coordinator was then to bring the trainee and trainer together to explain in full the training and development program for the next six months. The training designs contained theory and systems instruction, operational observations, self-paced learning, and hands-on operator training.

From the outset of the training and development phase, the personnel/training coordinators, none of whom had had experience with Middle Easterners before, were confronted with the problem of the nationals' motivation in the program. For example, the U.S. company placed a high value on safety regulations and personal safety on the job. While safety classes were given, the coordinators received continuous reports that the trainees were not complying with the rules. This was not limited to the plant environment—automobile accidents among the trainees were twelve times more frequent than among a comparable group of U.S. trainees.

The personnel/training coordinators attempted to counsel each trainee on safety, both personal and professional. However, while the trainees showed that they understood and agreed to comply with the safety regulations, violations continued. In the counseling sessions, problems of money and equitable compensation were discussed, and the Middle Eastern trainees felt they were underpaid and receiving less than others in the group. The compensation given to each trainee had been agreed upon in advance in his own country and set by the national joint venture partner prior to coming to the United States. While the compensation system did have differing pay levels, the overseas living allowance was the same for all. The coordinators observed a growing number of personal financial management problems among the trainees, who claimed the compensation did not adequately meet their needs. At the same time, the coordinators saw them buying new cars, moving into more expensive apartments, and frequenting the best restaurants and clubs in the area.

The Morning Meeting

As the training and development program progressed toward the halfway point, the number of unhappy trainees increased sharply, and four of the fifty returned home. At the initiative of the project's top U.S. management, a one-day meeting was held for selected American managers going to the host country to work on the project, the U.S. plant site coordinators, and the U.S. plant site trainers from the five U.S. plant locations. Including the in-country U.S. managing director, twenty-seven managers attended the morning meeting.

The coordinators and trainers discovered that their perceptions of the trainees, summarized below, coincided: (1) The trainees were arrogant and "peacockish" with a strong need for role and status. (2) The trainees were unwilling to take responsibility for their own growth and development. (3) The trainees were lazy and unwilling to take initiative. (4) The trainees talked much but accomplished little. (5) The trainees were afraid to roll up their sleeves and do things with their hands. (6) The trainees were excellent at mathematics and theoretical engineering but poor on practical applications. (7) The trainees were convinced that having a degree was enough and that continuing education was not necessary.

The trainers had more direct contact with the trainees during the three months of their training and development program. They were concerned about the trainees' varying responses to the four phases of instruction—namely, theory and systems instruction, operational observations, self-paced learning, and hands-on operator training, as follows:

Theory and Systems Instruction

The trainees preferred the theoretical to the systems portion. They liked the lectures but would not verbally participate in the training sessions. They liked to be tested on their notes but not on outside readings. They preferred to work on class projects and homework as a group. The trainees wanted the right answer on an examination and were frustrated by open-ended questions with no perfect answer. They wanted to call the instructors by their last names and were uncomfortable on a first-name basis. The trainers could not relax or become informal without losing their position of authority and respect in the eyes of the trainees. The trainees were proud of the source of their degrees and were apt to remind trainers and other trainees of it. Generally, the trainees' examination scores were within one point of being the same, and the informal leader of the group had the top score. The trainees continually complained about the eight-hour workday and the fast pace of the training schedule. When the plants instituted a heat conservation program, the trainees complained and petitioned to have the temperature raised from 65 degrees to the original temperature.

Operational Observations

The trainees wanted continuous dialogue among their class-mates to the distraction of the equipment operators and the trainers. They resisted breaking up into one-on-one training sessions and preferred to be in a group with the other trainees. Often, they were tardy for training sessions at the plants because of excessive socializing among themselves. They continually violated plant safety regulations while in the plant operating areas. When tested on operational observations, the trainees were adept at describing the systems, but poor at troubleshooting and problem solving. The trainers were very cautious not to embarrass a trainee in front of other trainees by asking him difficult questions.

Self-Paced Learning

The trainees did not like self-paced learning, because it took them away from other members of the group. They required considerable one-on-one trainer support to make the self-paced learning system work, and were reluctant to take individual initiative for their own learning. The trainees resented the practical content of the self-paced learning systems. In troubleshooting exercises in the self-paced learning system, they were frustrated without a list of solutions that could be memorized. If one member of the group of trainees progressed faster than the others in the group, peer pressure was exerted for him to slow down or be ostracized from the trainee group. Trainees continually wanted to negotiate time, schedules, and work pace with the trainers. Where self-paced learning involved a machine requiring manual dexterity and the use of small tools, trainees showed considerable stress.

Hands-On Operator Training

Trainees felt a loss of status once they started working with operators in the plant, feeling they were more educated than their American counterpart operators. Many of the trainees lacked the diagnostic skills to solve the problems that arose during their work on a particular system. Instructing the foreign trainees in identification and use of small tools took three times as long as for a comparable U.S. group. When technical problems with a system or machine interrupted the production flow, the trainees stepped aside to let the operator solve the problem instead of solving it themselves. The trainee absentee rate increased sharply in all plants during the hands-on period when the systems diagnostic and problem-solving period began.

Despite these problems with trainee performance, about 70 percent of the rural plant trainees and 50 percent of the urban plant trainees were at or above the training and development objectives set. As the overall goal, however, was to ameliorate the performance of the remaining trainees, a major portion of the meeting was devoted to discussions aimed at improving their training and development in the United States and ensuring that all returned to their home country with the skills needed to carry on a high-technology operation. When conversation turned to descriptions of what an ideal trainee should be, the resulting characterization depicted a typical American trainee. A more important aspect of the discussion, however, centered upon the kind of management organization which would result in the host country once the U.S., national, and third-country managers were all together.

Since the project was to be fully nationalized (managed and owned by nationals) in five years, a minority of those at the meeting argued that the joint venture company developed in the host country would be closer to a Middle Eastern organization. They argued that the resulting organization would have a high centralization of authority and responsibility at the top, the implication being that orders and directives would come from the top without any discussion, questioning, or participation from the subordinate personnel. Others argued that such a system of management would not work, given the highly decentralized nature of the technology and the individual performance requirements in the specific subsystems. Individual initiative, acceptance of authority and responsibility, and effective monitoring of individual and group goals were essential, they argued, if the total high-technology system was to operate efficiently. They further argued that heavy participation and involvement through superior-subordinate and peer-peer communications was necessary if the interdependent subsystems were to work effectively. A clearer picture of their own company management philosophy was explored in contrast to that of a typical firm in the country of their joint venture.

The U.S. company worked on the principle that if effective planning, budgeting, and control were exercised, an individual or group could monitor its own performance through the feedback system. As the individual or group goals were contained in the planning and budgeting system, either new goals were established or corrective action was taken. If new goals were established, they would then be communicated along with the plan for implementing them. The plan would be put into effect and the goals monitored, thus completing the management cycle. A final principle was the measurement of the manager's performance. In the U.S. company the managers were given specific criteria through which their performance could be measured. These criteria were:

Cost control: Low per-unit cost; ability to plan as well as control one's budget; ability to maintain profit-center profitability; ability to cope with budgeted variances.

Quality assurance: Quality control systems instituted to ensure the highest quality at the lowest cost; monitoring of statistical quality control procedures and systems for deviations; upgrading systems to ensure the highest quality for the lowest per-unit cost.

Work environment: Cleanliness of work spaces to ensure a high-quality control environment and employee satisfaction; work spaces layed out in accordance with employee efficiency, safety requirements and plant cleanliness.

Organization development: Effective interpersonal communications directed toward organization's goals; motivation of individuals toward organization's objectives; development of employee potential; fair exercise of discipline; low absenteeism; low turnover.

Safety: Proper indoctrination of personnel in safety regulations; reduction and control of accidents; removal of cause of accidents.

Many at the meeting questioned the appropriateness of the U.S. company's philosophy, principles, and managerial performance criteria in light of some of the problems encountered with the trainees in the five U.S. plants. This was further complicated by the results of a survey in the same Middle Eastern country taken by an organization development specialist concerning a similar high-technology joint venture with another American company. In Table 1 it can be seen that the attitudes of the Middle Eastern and Western

Table 1

I. ADJECTIVES SELECTED BY HOST COUNTRY NATIONALS TO DESCRIBE WESTERNERS

a.	Arrogant	g.	They are not sociable locally
b.	Reserved	h.	Experienced, but not knowledgeable
c.	Objective, not flexible		(trained, but not educated)
d.	Some lack of confidence in host country nationals	i.	Superiority feeling
e.	Honest	j.	Uncoordinated
f.	They know their business but do not admit mistakes	k.	Loyal

II. ADJECTIVES PREDICTED BY WESTERNERS AS BEING THOSE THE HOST COUNTRY NATIONALS WOULD SELECT TO DESCRIBE WESTERNERS

a.	Proud	r.	Naive
b.	Devious	s.	Weak
c.	Overbearing	t.	Wasteful
d.	Inefficient	u.	Indecisive
e.	Know-it-all	v.	Selfish
f.	Impatient	w.	Aggressive
g.	Rude	x.	Demanding
h.	Clanning	y.	Motivated by money
i.	Immoral	z.	Lack of understanding of host country nationals' way
j.	Overpaid		
k.	Pedantic	aa.	Looking down on host country nationals
l.	Incapable		
m.	Untrusting	bb.	Not diplomatic
n.	Discriminatory	cc.	Pushy
o.	Cold/Aloof	dd.	Stupid
p.	Friendly	ee.	Knowledgeable
q.	Salient	ff.	Inflexible

III. ADJECTIVES SELECTED BY WESTERNERS TO DESCRIBE HOST COUNTRY NATIONALS

a.	Hesitant to ask for directions	o.	No sense of urgency
b.	Two-faced	p.	Masters of passive resistance
c.	Slow	q.	Dishonest
d.	Kind	r.	Striving
e.	Hospitable	s.	Status seeking
f.	Jovial	t.	Emotional
g.	Good-natured	u.	Proud
h.	Individualistic	v.	Secretive
i.	Clever	w.	Receptive
j.	Energetic	x.	Elusive
k.	Sensitive	y.	Not willing to accept responsibility
l.	Lack of drive/motivation		
m.	Forgetful	z.	Find it difficult to delegate
n.	Require constant follow up	aa.	Suspicious

IV. ADJECTIVES PREDICTED BY HOST COUNTRY NATIONALS AS BEING THOSE THE WESTERNERS WOULD SELECT TO DESCRIBE HOST COUNTRY NATIONALS

a.	Incapable	d.	Emotional
b.	Inefficient	e.	Shrewd
c.	Honesty questionable	f.	Untrusting

managers toward one another hindered the joint venture in performing effectively as an operating unit. With these data, the meeting broke for lunch with the clear understanding that what they did in the afternoon session, and indeed throughout the remaining three months of training, would dramatically affect the kind of organization that would result.

7
International Resources Corporation: Dealing with Powerful Host Country Nationals

John Seifert

The case study illustrates the interaction between an international company and powerful host country nationals concerning arrangements for modern office space for the company. The difficulty of planning in a situation of unprecedented growth is illustrated as well. The case shows that affiliation with powerful local interest is a double-edged sword which can be used both in favor of and against an international company. Among the issues raised in this case are these: (1) The international company attempts to function according to internationally acceptable standards of service which may not be consistent with the levels deemed desirable by a particular country. (2) The company, especially at the headquarters level, seeks a clear statement of rules and regulations allowing for irrevocable and legally binding commitment. This approach is often at odds with the prevailing business context and creates significant conflict. (3) The nature and scope of the role and responsibilities of a company are determined less by normally accepted definitions than by the context of operations in a country.

In this case, note the similarities and differences in the negotiating styles of International Resources Corporation and Mr. Mansour and consider the reasons for these differences. Consider also how Hogan can determine the real reasons for a lack of a response from the appropriate government official and whether Mansour's assistance should be sought.

* * *

International Resources Corporation (IRC) maintained a branch operation in an oil-producing Middle Eastern country (Islamaland) from the late 1960s. Its principal activity was to offer various financial and nonfinancial services to importing and trading houses which served about half of the country. A majority of the senior staff of the office, with the exception of one or two expatriates in the positions of manager and senior operations officer who normally stayed only one or two years, had been with the company for more than five years. The business had grown gradually over the years. In early 1970, IRC opened a new office in the capital of the country which rapidly grew to about 150 percent of the size of the older office, primarily because the early stages of the economic boom were concentrated in the capital. However, after 1973, the rate of growth of the older branch accelerated sharply, benefiting from major new construction and industrial activity in addition to growth in the traditional importing and trading sector.

The older office building had been built in 1950. It was a two-story, flat-roofed structure clad with grey stucco, constructed to the unambitious standards of the country long before the boom. The office premises had never been up to IRC's standards for overseas premises, and received rock-bottom rating in this category when inspected in 1974. The booming economy drew more attention and more visitors to the area, and individuals from the European head office returned with poor impressions of this branch which became known as "the pit."

The staff of the IRC office increased from 90 in 1974 to 160 by early 1975, and stopgap measures were being taken to create space. Inactive files were moved to a storefront in a low-rent residential district to create an area for new marketing officers. New clerical staff were accommodated by a newly constructed mezzanine over the high-ceilinged lobby. The current joke was that the next step would be a large tent on the roof.

Because of the crowding, working conditions in the twenty-five-year-old building deteriorated rapidly. Circulation was increasingly difficult, and departments became intermingled, resulting in confusion of work flows and headaches for supervisors. Complaints about the overloaded sanitary facilities were frequent. Gradually, breakdowns spread to virtually every area—the electrical system, the telephone system, plumbing, air conditioning; even the main doors became overworked and subject to frequent breakdowns. Working conditions at IRC were alarmingly poor, with no relief in sight.

Because parking had become impossible in the congested area around the office, clients visited less frequently, preferring to do business by messenger. Management endured clients' complaints at every social function.

Because the basic problem, aside from lack of space, was the old age of the building, little could be done to improve working conditions without unacceptable disruptions or even a lengthy shutdown for a major overhaul. IRC's manager in the country became aware that working conditions were having a serious impact on morale.

The market for local staff was extremely competitive due to the rise in salary scales of 50 percent per annum. Competing organizations were making major inroads into IRC's market in the country partly because they provided more pleasant working conditions. IRC was a source of experienced bilingual clerical staff in the area, and it suffered employee losses because of the much higher salaries paid by international construction companies and engineering firms coming to the country. Regarding salary, IRC could not compete with construction companies with two-year cost-plus contracts, but its management felt that job security, fringe benefits, and working conditions were areas in which it could outweigh the competition.

IRC's organization in Islamaland had not prepared for rapid growth. No one was charged with general responsibility for the office premises, and premises planning had never been part of the annual planning and budgeting cycle, except for quick estimates of rents and utilities. In the absence of a consistent monitoring of premises requirements as a part of the annual planning cycle, the few expansions and improvements which had been made had been personal efforts of several expatriate managers. Because each of the expatriates expected to stay no more than two years, there had been little incentive to consider a long-term, high-cost capital project such as a new office. Other evidence of little incentive was that the growth rate only two years earlier had been so unimpressive that a long-term lease on a compound of six houses for expatriate managers had been allowed to expire.

The problems of inadequate space, poor working conditions, low morale among employees, and discontented clients were visibly acute, and the poor inspection rating of the physical premises in late 1974 confirmed them. The European headquarters sought specific recommendations for improving the premises. Second only to performance against budget, inspection ratings were the key standard against which management was evaluated in IRC, and operations officers' careers depended on them.

In June 1975, IRC held a general review of results and long-term plans in the effort to improve its inspection rating. In attendance were the senior vice-president in charge of the Middle East, country manager Robert Hogan, and James Jones, who was in charge of office operations. Although some progress had been made, crowding, low morale, and customer complaints continued. Jones recommended that investigations be made whether a third floor could be added to the building. Hogan approved expenditures for architectural and engineering studies.

As these studies proceeded over the next several weeks, James Jones began negotiations with the building's owner, Sheik Abdullah. The current lease had another six years to run at a cost of $3.40 per square foot. The sheik, who would not consider making any contribution to the cost of adding a floor to his building, demanded that the lease be renegotiated to reflect current rental levels of about $35 per square foot in return for his permission to add the third floor.

By mid-August, the architectural and engineering studies had shown that the floor could be added at a cost of $2 million, which came as a shock on top of the prospective increase in rent. Further consultation with the IRC's premises staff in Europe, particularly a British construction consultant, convinced Jones that there would be serious disruptions and potential delays in constructing the third floor, and that the additional space would be adequate only to accommodate the staff projected for mid-year 1976. Since the floor would take nearly a year to complete, Jones saw that they would be facing the same situation again a year later, without the option of adding another floor, which, the studies showed, the building would not support. A consensus emerged among the local executives of IRC that the poor visibility of the office, the lack of parking in the area, the overloading of utilities and day-long traffic jams in the downtown area made expansion of the existing premises, at high cost, an unattractive proposition.

Through a local architect friend, Jones was able to obtain information from the municipal planning office which indicated that the congested and overloaded conditions in the downtown area would only grow worse during the next several years. Clients were complaining that they were spending over an hour in traffic to reach IRC's office. The three telephone lines at the office were so inadequate that clients had to spend up to two days getting through to the office. Frequent interruptions of water and power service forced Jones to resort to manual bookkeeping when the office computer was out of service and to having water delivered by private suppliers from thirty miles away.

Hogan was under pressure from two local groups to reduce IRC's presence in the country. He also knew that these groups had considerable influence with powerful government officials. Hogan felt that a public relations campaign emphasizing IRC's commitment to the development of the local economy would tend to reduce pressure on IRC. IRC's profits in the country, although at about $24 million in 1975, were rumored to be several times larger. Officials were said to feel that IRC was too dominating a presence since it seemed to have all major local and foreign names as its clients. Hogan felt that acquiring new premises would be another way for IRC to express its commitment to the country. Hogan's opinion, coupled with Jones' growing pessimism concerning the additional floor as a solution to IRC's problems, resulted in the contracting of a British real estate consulting firm to study and recommend potential sites for a new branch.

Though recommendations from this firm included several possible sites, none could be developed in less than three years. Most of the sites would have involved acquiring two or more contiguous parcels, a situation certain to produce extortionate costs and delays. The local area was already one of the most expensive real estate markets in the world, with prime commercial sites priced between $3 million and $4 million per acre. In September, Hogan formed a committee of IRC officers to search for other possible locations which could be developed more quickly and at lower cost.

One of the committee members, Steve Hemlock, had been working closely with the shipping subsidiary of the state oil company and had become acquainted with Mr. Mansour, a key decision maker in the oil company. Mansour was constructing, as a personal investment, an eleven-story commercial, office, and apartment building covering a full block in a quiet area of embassies and large residences near one of two major streets leading into the downtown area of the city. It was reported that Mansour would be willing to negotiate with IRC for a lease for a new office location in his building.

The search for a new site had proceeded on the assumption that a parcel of land would be purchased and a building constructed on it for the sole use of IRC. Although ownership of land by foreign corporations for the conduct of normal business activities was permitted under country commercial law, case-by-case approval of the Ministry of Commerce and Industry was required. In two previous cases, when land was purchased for expatriate housing, obtaining approval had taken more than a year. The prospect of leasing space for the new office eliminated this major complication, which had forced previous land purchases to be executed in the name of certain local officers of IRC pending ministerial approvals.

It had been rumored in IRC offices that one of these local officers, who had held title to the bank's expatriate housing compound in the capital for several years, had at one time considered selling the compound to a third party. He had joined IRC long before from a respected family. Because his father was a respected general, he was highly valued for his ability to gain favors for IRC from high levels in the government and royal family. However, he was not highly regarded as a manager and had seen his local contemporaries rise to much more prestigious positions in the government. Shortly after a quick visit by the officer in charge of the region, title to the compound was returned to IRC, and the local officer was given a promotion.

Leasing a new location presented problems as well. The country had a small, closed society where business and politics were concerned. Association with a given landlord could imply more than a simple lessor-lessee relationship, since a landlord might be viewed also as a patron whose relative success or failure would condition IRC's prestige, influence, and access to important figures in business and government. All these factors were important since key decisions were not made by legislative or judicial process but through patterns of influence based on family and business associations and mutual interest.

In early October, Jones had been given the responsibility for all of IRC's premises and housing activities in the country. His preliminary review of Mansour's building showed it to be highly satisfactory. The building offered sufficient space to accommodate the growth of the office for several years. The location and attractive architecture of the building would lend the prestige that the current premises lacked, and the area offered automobile access and parking, both practically nonexistent at the current location. Most important, the building's reinforced concrete structure was complete and it could be occupied in about a year. Jones learned as well that IRC had been instrumental in organizing and participating in loans to Mansour for the major portion of the building's financing, which might give the IRC an inside track in negotiating a lease. (IRC had decided a year earlier to help Mansour because of the association it provided to a powerful individual who could help in numerous ways.)

In early October, senior area management and Hogan gave their preliminary approval of the location. They were particularly pleased with the possibility of cementing IRC's relations with Mansour, who was thought to be an important contact for IRC. As a key official of the state oil company reporting to the minister of petroleum, Mansour controlled rapidly growing volumes of spot oil sales. Financial intermediation of these sales of as much as $10 million each generated substantial fees and fund float, which represented a major potential source of IRC earnings, if more of the business could be directed to IRC. Mansour was also a controlling factor in the downstream development of the country's petroleum sector, which would represent billions of dollars in capital expenditures. Project finance advisory service and lending seemed to be enormous opportunities for IRC if it could gain access to the decision makers, who were courted by a stream of major oil company executives and investment bankers.

A leading international oil company was negotiating with the state oil company for the establishment of a plant to produce lubricating oil, which was in short supply in the country, and saw this venture as a means to ensure its access to Islamaland's crude oil and markets after the nationalization of foreign oil companies in the country was completed. The oil company had put a company jet at Mansour's disposal and had flown in scores of videotaped movies for his entertainment. Videotape was a prime source of entertainment in the country, although it was virtually impossible to clear recorded tape through customs. Since films were also forbidden, videotapes of U.S. television programs and movies were in great demand among host country nationals like Mansour who had been educated in the West.

Mansour's control of the country's oil sector was by no means absolute, however. The Ministry of Planning had a group of petroleum industry experts from the American Research Institute developing plans for the downstream development of the petroleum sector. When the head of the Ministry of Planning learned in early 1974 that Mansour had retained an American consulting firm to do a parallel plan, he privately accused the state oil company of attempting to usurp his authority over national planning. Consequently, the American consulting firm's efforts shifted to a study of internal organization at the state oil company, and later, the consulting firm's staff left the country.

In October, before beginning negotiations with Mansour, Jones and the British construction consultant who flew in from London prepared a feasibility study of the proposed new branch. Preliminary floor plans for the branch were prepared, using blueprints which had been submitted in connection with the financing of the building. A firm of British structural and mechanical engineers was employed to determine the adequacy of the designed air conditioning system and the building's ability to support vaults and masses of files. A study of the current market rent level was prepared. Although other rental space was available, no other location could offer the 43,000 square feet required for the new office. Because IRC's business in the country was growing at about 200 percent per year, budgets were revised quarterly. Since organizational growth had been lagging behind business growth for about two years, each revision showed a major increase in numbers of staff. Consequently, space requirements for the new office were to rise constantly during the negotiations with Mansour, finally reaching 55,000 square feet. Calculations prepared by Jones and the British consultant based on IRC's standards for overseas offices showed that the existing space was, at 9,000 square feet, only half the size actually required; and projected growth in staff plus addition of a new computer, employees' club, and training and mechanical facilities would cause the size of the branch to quadruple over five years.

By early November, Jones and the consultant had agreed with Hogan on preliminary plans for the new branch. Space was selected on the first three floors of the building for the various departments. The engineers had reported that the building would be structurally adequate, and that sufficient air conditioning could be arranged within the designed system. In order to ensure that the new office would be completed on schedule and according to IRC standards, it was decided that IRC would do a major portion of the work on its areas of the building. IRC's architect, who had performed work for it throughout the Middle East, would prepare the designs and it was thought that the prime contractor on the building, a local firm with a Lebanese partner, might be used to perform the work. It was agreed that a market rent level of about $18 per square foot would be used as a basis of negotiation. A target date of January 1977 was set for occupying the new office, allowing three months for negotiation of the lease and ten months for construction.

Jones would attempt to negotiate a rebate of IRC's cost of construction against the rentals to be agreed upon with Mansour. A fifteen-year lease was thought to be the maximum obtainable.

In mid-November 1975, Hogan and Jones met Mansour for the first time. The meeting was held at Mansour's private apartment in the capital of Islamaland in the housing compound of a U.S. consulting firm assisting the state oil company in planning refinery operations. (Throughout the subsequent negotiations, Mansour rarely had anyone negotiating with him. Persons familiar with his negotiating style confirmed that he was highly secretive and preferred to negotiate alone.)

At this first meeting, Jones found Mansour to be soft-spoken, articulate, and imposing despite his short stature and undistinguished, round, bespectacled face. His schoolmaster manner made Jones wonder how flexible Mansour would be in the negotiations. After Hogan explained to Mansour that Jones would be responsible for negotiating the prospective lease, Jones outlined IRC's space requirements, and stated that market rent levels appeared to be in the order of $18 per square foot. IRC would like as long-term a lease as possible, perhaps fifteen years. Mansour replied that the space requirements could be met, but that he had already rented certain areas at $30 per square foot, and could not consider renting a substantial portion of his building at much lower rates. He did volunteer, however, that the presence of IRC offices in his building would make it attractive, and he consequently agreed to consider a lease as long as twenty-five years. Jones arranged to meet with Mansour's architect to discuss details of IRC's requirements.

When Jones met with the architect a few days later, he learned that details for the completion of the building were unclear. The architectural office in Beirut where the building was designed had been destroyed in the Lebanese civil war, and the completion of designs and specifications for finishing stages of the building had been halted. While work on basic walls, plumbing, and electrical aspects could continue, it would be several months before the architect would complete the final designs for floors, ceilings, windows, plumbing, and lighting fixtures. From the architect's comments on the current pace of construction, Jones surmised that the contractor was incurring cost overruns due to inflation and was delaying work in an attempt to force renegotiation of his contract.

William Hartley of IRC had negotiated the original financial package for the building with Mansour. Shortly after the meeting between Jones and Mansour's architect, Hartley informed Jones that he had been approached by a representative of Mansour for additional financing, citing price rises for construction materials. Hartley could not arrange an increase without approval from headquarters in Europe. Jones secured Hogan's approval to offer Mansour advances of rent in exchange for a reduction in rent rates and periodic (preferably five-year) rental reviews. The advance of funds, which were readily available in the market at 3 percent per annum, would not represent a significant cost to IRC, and the risk of the building not being completed was controlled under the financing agreements. In addition, the delay and complication of seeking additional credit approvals from headquarters could be avoided. It was also concluded that, in view of the delay in completing designs for the building, IRC should prepare plans and cost estimates for completion of its space, taking the present status as a starting point. A telex was sent telling the British consultant in London to prepare cost estimates for the next regional planning conference in London in mid-December. Jones would also be required to present estimates of rental costs and basic lease terms for the approval of senior officers.

Jones contacted Mansour to request a meeting, and was invited to his home a few days later. Jones knew that this invitation was counter to local ideas of privacy and Mansour's secretiveness, and interpreted it as a positive signal. When they met, Jones was able to obtain reduction of rental rates for the three floors of the building to an average $16 per square foot, in return for advance of two years' rent to be paid in stages over the course of completion of construction. When Jones proposed rent reviews every five years, Mansour proposed ten years. A compromise was struck at seven years, in return for advance of a third year's rent. Jones then raised the question of rebating IRC's construction cost against the rentals. Mansour seemed to feel he had been tricked. Jones quickly explained IRC's concern with the delays in construction, saying that IRC contemplated making a major investment which would enhance the appearance and value of the building. Mansour reluctantly agreed to some rebating but insisted on using his original contractual costs for the works rather than actual cost to IRC. Since he would be traveling for most of the next several months, he was eager to see a draft of the lease. Jones replied that negotiation of the rebates ought to be the first priority since this information would be required for submitting final documentation for approval by headquarters. Mansour agreed to this last point, and informed Jones that he would be in London at the time of IRC's regional planning conference. Jones agreed to call on him to inform him of the outcome of the presentation for the new branch.

The London presentation went well, but two senior executives were opposed to using IRC's usual architect for the job. Several projects in the Middle East under that firm's supervision were complicated by delays and cost overruns, and the architect's fees had become excessive. The head of premises and the British consultant were asked to request fee bids from reliable firms in London and Amsterdam. The preliminary estimates of $3.5 million for construction, to be amortized in annual rent over an average life of fifteen years, were approved, and the consultant was instructed to proceed with final cost estimates using the IRC's usual architect on a provisional basis. A target date for submission of the final report to headquarters was set for late December.

Jones went to Mansour's hotel in London to inform him of the outcome, but the desk denied he was there. After finally persuading the concierge to inform Mansour of his presence, Jones met Mansour over coffee in the lobby and learned that a secret OPEC meeting was in progress. Jones brought Mansour up to date and Mansour informed him that he would be vacationing in Egypt until late in January.

Soon after returning to Islamaland, Jones learned that at the previous week's meeting of the Council of Ministers it had been decided to strip the state oil company of its authority over downstream development of the petroleum sector. A new Ministry of Electricity and Industry would control this area. Nothing further was heard concerning Mansour's position in the new arrangement, as all business and government activity came to a halt for three weeks during the Muslim pilgrimage to Mecca and Medina, the hajj. Later, in mid-January, an editorial was published in a leading local newspaper concerning Mansour's building. It stated that the building, at nine stories, was in violation of the six-story zoning limit for its area. Further, Mansour was attacked for adding three floors to a six-story building, making it structurally unsafe.

Jones visited the construction site and found it abandoned. A guard informed him that municipal authorities had ordered construction stopped and had seized a quantity of equipment. Jones' contact at the Municipal Planning Office told him that the office had originally agreed to turn a blind eye to the zoning violation, but that "things had changed." Jones' consulting engineers insisted the building was safe, and that their calculations showed it had originally been designed for nine stories.

The editorial attack on a senior government official was unprecedented. Hogan, Jones, and other senior expatriate IRC officers agreed that there might be an effort under way by Mansour's rivals in the government to drive Mansour out of power and possibly out of the country. IRC's senior government relations officer in Islamaland made inquiries and said that while it was not clear what was happening, it was unlikely that Mansour would be completely stripped of power, since this was not the way in which host country nationals handled conflict. In any case, IRC had no alternatives to waiting and seeing what would happen with its premises.

Mansour returned to Islamaland's capital briefly in late January. He invited Jones to his home, and expressed confidence that the zoning problem would be resolved. It seemed that a senior municipality official, who was notorious for self-enrichment by permitting zoning deviations, was also being chastised.

Although Mansour was in Geneva, Paris, London, New York, and Cairo for most of the next two months, Jones proceeded to draft the lease, to which Mansour readily agreed during brief visits to Islamaland. In mid-February senior management approved the project budget and plan for submission to headquarters. A Dutch architectural firm was selected to design the branch.

By May, Mansour was at home, and construction had resumed on the lower floors of the building. One of Mansour's deputies, whom he also used as a personal assistant, told Jones that a compromise, possibly a fine, was being negotiated on the upper three floors, which would eventually be completed. Space requirements for the new IRC offices had twice been revised upward, and the new architects found that IRC would have to install its own air conditioning system and that three diesel generators would have to be installed in the building's basement. These additions resulted in a substantial increase in cost above the level submitted for approval in the plan to headquarters.

Jones, the consultant, and the architects met with Mansour in late May in an office at the construction site. Mansour, visibly impressed with the architect's graphic presentation of plans for the interior and exterior of the new branch, requested his assistance in planning the exterior marble cladding and windows for the lower levels of the entire building. His own architect, cut off from his design office in Beirut, had made little progress in final designs. IRC's architects also volunteered assistance with certain mechanical systems in the building, including the garbage compaction system. They feared that otherwise the building's basement would fill with refuse from the garbage chutes.

As discussion of details progressed, Mansour was brought up to a level of $9.1 million in construction costs to be incurred by IRC and rebated against rent, where he stood firm. The consultant continued to bombard Mansour with further details justifying his higher estimate. Knowing that Mansour's political eclipse was ending, and sensing that an explosion point was approaching between the consultant and Mansour, Jones terminated the discussion and confirmed that the rebate would be $9.1 million.

The lease was completed, sent to headquarters for legal approval, and signed in late June 1976, but not before one final issue was resolved. Hogan had known since the fall of 1975 that IRC would have to seek approval of two government agencies to relocate its offices. However, because of the sensitivity about IRC's dominant position and the uncertainty of Mansour's political position, application for approval had not been made.

The key official in the agency (with greater importance in approving applications) died in early 1976, and the attitude of his successor was unknown. By May, Hogan had met on several occasions with the new official and he felt confident that approval for relocation could be obtained. A letter explaining IRC's intentions and requesting approval was sent to the second-level official. Two weeks passed. Inquiries as to the status of IRC's application received the reply that, since the letter had been addressed to the second-level official, the first-level official would not sign his approval. A delegation of IRC executives went to make apologies. Approval might be forthcoming, they were told, but IRC must confirm that the existing office space would be closed as soon as the new premises were in operation. The confirmation was sent and a letter of approval was received soon after.

Construction of the new premises began in July, using a British contractor selected by competitive bidding in May.

Kuwait in Kiawah: Arab Direct Investment in the United States

William Stoever

This case concerns an attempted marriage between Arab oil wealth and American managerial expertise in an American investment opportunity. The marriage was intended to produce a luxury resort complex on an island off the South Carolina coast. Financing—some $150 million to $250 million—was to come from the Kuwait Investment Company, which was jointly owned by the Kuwait government and approximately 5,000 private shareholders. Construction and managerial and marketing expertise were to be supplied by the Sea Pines Company, which had previously successfully developed a resort complex on South Carolina's Hilton Head Island. From the Kuwaiti viewpoint the investment provided a way to put excess capital to use, cut down dependence on the single commodity of oil, and expand their rate of return beyond portfolio investment. For the South Carolinians the Kuwaiti investment was a response to their vigorous efforts to attract foreign direct investment and a chance for a renewed stimulus to a part of the state which had long been stagnant and backward. But the venture ran into opposition even before construction was undertaken, and the partnership

---

This case is based upon a study of court documents and depositions, contractual records and planning studies, extensive news articles and other secondary sources, and interviews with many of the key participants in New York and South Carolina.

dissolved into suit and countersuit. This case examines the difficulties that arose and the efforts to resolve them. The case actually breaks down into two distinct parts: the environmentalist/ethnic opposition to the project, and the later lawsuit between the Kuwaitis and Sea Pines.

Some of the issues reflected in the case include the role of publicity in negotiations, the desire of the foreign investor to maintain a low profile, especially where the image of a nation is involved, and the overall package of resources sought by an Arab investor given its particular strengths and limitations.

In reading the case, consider the different approaches to negotiation of (both public and private) Kuwaiti and U.S. groups. In what ways and why did the issues of conflict change over time? Identify the catalyst in this project and the factors contributing to its success or failure. What specific course of action would you recommend that Kuwaiti interests pursue in order to ensure effective control over the operations?

*   *   *

The Kuwait government incorporated the Kuwait Investment Company, S.A.K., to facilitate its search for and management of overseas investments. Two Kuwaiti citizens, Abdlatif al Hamad and Bader al Dawood, were installed as president and chief deputy, respectively. One of their chief advisors was an American named Richard Williamson, who had been loaned to the government of Kuwait by the World Bank in 1969 and had stayed on as an employee of Kuwait Investment Company. The investment company's major resource was money; it did not have technological or managerial skills to contribute to projects. Therefore, the Kuwaitis wanted investments that required extensive capital without much supervision on their part. Real estate seemed to be a logical choice because of the heavy initial capital requirements, the possibility of hiring host-country citizens to manage it, and the potential for lucrative returns if the development was successful. In addition, investment in real estate might stir up less controversy than had been encountered with earlier Arab investments in American and European banks and manufacturing industries.

Richard Williamson, a native South Carolinian, first awakened the Kuwaitis' interest in Kiawah (pronounced KEE-a-wuh) Island. The island had one of the few remaining undeveloped beaches on the east coast of the United States. Such beach front was much in demand, and the prices had risen dramatically in recent years. The island lay some twenty miles south of Charleston, South Carolina, within Charleston County. It was zoned for "general agricultural" use. This classification would have allowed subdividing the entire island into plots for one-family houses, but it did not allow construction of commercial or multiple-occupancy dwellings. Kiawah Island was owned by the heirs of a man who had bought it for logging operations in 1951. It was virtually uninhabited, although others of the so-called "sea islands" were inhabited by low-income black subsistence farmers. The islands were also known as "barrier islands" because they form a natural barrier protecting the mainland from Atlantic Ocean storms and high waves. While the beaches on many of the islands were receding because the sand was being swept out to sea, the beach on Kiawah was stable. Ecologists say the island has a uniquely rich and varied ecosystem. It is covered with a lush semitropical growth of palm trees, tall grasses, and loblolly pines hanging with Spanish moss. It abounds with wildlife: deer, alligators, hogs, and several species of rare birds. In June and July, giant seagoing loggerhead turtles come onto its beaches to lay their eggs.

Williamson advised the Kuwaitis to keep their interest in Kiawah Island confidential while conducting negotiations to buy it.

Kuwait Investment Company incorporated an American subsidiary, Coastal Shores, Inc., and hired a lawyer from South Carolina to represent its interests. Even so, rumors of the negotiations leaked out in early 1973, including wild stories that the Kuwaitis planned to build an oil refinery on the island or were building up an arms stockpile there. In June 1973 Williamson found it advisable to inform the Charleston newspapers that the deal had not been consummated and that there never had been any intention of putting a refinery on the island. He said:

> Had our plans been successful, our intention all along was to make Kiawah the most prestigious resort on the Atlantic Coast . . . Kuwait leaders were looking forward 25 to 30 years to the time when oil supplies may have been depleted or new fuels developed to replace petroleum. We essentially are interested in real estate development on a long-term basis as an income producer to take up the slack when and if oil ceases to be profitable.

Further difficulties arose when several members of the owner's family made clear their opposition to selling the island to Arabs, especially after the Arab oil boycott of mid-1973 forced long lines at American gasoline pumps.

Williamson advised the Kuwaitis not to make a final commitment to purchase the island until they had lined up a suitable developer to oversee design and construction of the resort complex. He approached Charles Fraser, founder and (at that time) president of Sea Pines Company. Fraser had been the guiding genius behind Sea Pines Company's successful development of a luxury resort called Sea Pines Plantation on Hilton Head Island, off the South Carolina coast just north of Savannah, Georgia. Fraser had won several awards from real estate organizations for tasteful development and preservation of the environment on Sea Pines Plantation, but he had a reputation for overspending, and he had started several new projects which were spreading Sea Pines' resources thin.

The Kuwaitis were close to a final deal for purchase of Kiawah Island in January 1974. According to Fraser, the Kuwaitis' lawyer said they would not go through with the purchase unless Sea Pines agreed to be their development partner. Fraser said the main issue in the negotiations with

Sea Pines was how Kuwait Investment was going to compen-
sate Sea Pines for the time and expertise of its top management, including all the strategy planning, marketing techniques, financial models, and computer programs that Sea
Pines had developed in the past seventeen years. Sea Pines
wanted a lump-sum payment of $2 million to $3 million in
advance plus several million more as services were performed.
Kuwait Investment desired to hold the front-end cash payments as low as possible until after cash was being produced.
Fraser was leery of the various schemes the Kuwaitis proposed
for profit-sharing. (He later recalled with irony that Bader
al Dawood assured him: "Trust us and we will be like
brothers.") Another question concerned the value to be
placed on the intangibles; Fraser claimed that Sea Pines'
expertise and guidance could enable Kiawah to start produc-
ing revenue within two or three years, instead of the four or
five years it would require for Kuwait Investment to hire,
train, and start into operation a staff of its own.

These issues were unresolved when, on February 15, a
formal announcement was made that the Kuwait Investment
Company had purchased Kiawah Island for $17,385,000.
This worked out to $4,500 per acre, which Williamson said
was not a bad price for eleven miles of prime beach frontage.
Initial reaction by the media to the sale was cautiously favor-
able; the Charleston *News and Courier* hoped that growing
interdependence between the Kuwaiti and American economies would make the Kuwaitis "more reasonable to deal
with" on oil and other matters. However, the paper called
for congressional research on the impact of foreign investment in the United States.

It was further announced that the Kuwaitis planned to
build a luxury resort on the island at a cost of some $150
million to $200 million and that they had retained the
Environmental Research Center of Columbia, South Carolina,
to conduct an environmental impact study of the proposed
development. The Environmental Research Center asked that

the fee of $200,000 be put in escrow so that the firm would be guaranteed payment as soon as it had completed the study, regardless of how complimentary or critical it was to the proposed development plans.

On March 15 the Kuwaitis' American lawyer announced that Sea Pines would be the developer of the Kiawah resort complex. A Charleston *Evening Post* editorial called the announcement "welcome assurance of good taste. Sea Pines Company . . . has already demonstrated its competence . . . in planning and administering high class resorts." The contract solved the problems of valuation and payment for services by dividing Sea Pines' management services into two categories:

1. "Central Services" was to consist of "approximately 250 persons as of February 15, 1974, including all central corporate officers and a management and professional staff including central accounting and computer services, research and management training, budget department, . . . communications productions, public relations, sales management, design and construction management, golf and outdoor sports management, executive services, and resort research." It was also supposed to include use of Sea Pines' budget forms, computer programs, financial models, econometric forecasting techniques for resort demand, and the like. The contract stated that the value of these services could not be accurately determined, so the Kiawah Island Company* (as Coastal Shores, Inc., had been renamed) would pay $1,200,000 annually, at the rate of $100,000 per month, on account of the central services.

2. Services provided by persons other than Central Services personnel would be charged on a professional, by-the-hour rate equal to 250 percent of the employee's base salary rate. An example is engineering and geology supervision by member companies which were separate entities from the Sea Pines parent company. Sea Pines was also to get a percentage of

---

*Also called Kiawah Beach Company.

the profits according to a sliding scale: 10 percent of the first $1 million, 33 percent of the next $4 million, and 50 percent of any annual profit above $5 million. In summary, Sea Pines was to receive (a) $100,000 per month, (b) 250 percent of the hourly salary rate of professional employees not included in the standard monthly allocation, and (c) a share of the profits.

As part of the contract, Sea Pines appended its annual statement for the fiscal year ended February 28, 1973, and its six-month statement ending August 31, 1973. The contract said: "Sea Pines warrants that . . . no material adverse changes have occurred . . . since . . . such statements." The contract also gave either party the right to terminate the contract in the event of default by the other, where "default" included "failure to perform . . . any material obligation set forth in this contract."

Sea Pines sent a management team headed by Frank W. Brumley, a former vice-president, to take charge of the Kiawah development. Williamson insisted that Brumley and his top assistants sever all connections with Sea Pines, including dropping out of the pension plan, in order to assure their complete loyalty to Kiawah Island Company. Fraser said he selected Brumley for the Kiawah position because he was articulate and good at the public relations skills needed to steer Kiawah Island through the desired zoning change. Brumley was named vice-president and general manager of the new company; president was Abdlatif al Hamad, the president of Kuwait Investment Company.

As soon as the Kiawah Island contract was signed, Fraser and his planners set vigorously to work on a master plan for the island's development. By the time of the first formal meeting of the management committee on June 19 and 20, they had produced a document entitled "Policy Statement No. 1: A Strategic Plan for Kiawah Island" and five technical reports. A lot of careful thinking apparently went into the plan. It projected a development period stretching over fifteen to twenty years resulting eventually in a series of "villages" strung along the island. The villages would be separated by green belts one-half mile or more wide on which the forest and underbrush would remain undisturbed. Although population and housing density would be fairly high within each village, overall density on the island would be kept fairly low. Lots, single-family dwellings, and condominiums would be sold. There were strict architectural requirements: designs had to be approved and most buildings had to be made of wood so that the architecture would blend in with the natural surroundings. As much as possible of the original forest was to be preserved. Each village would be essentially completed before the next was started. Since construction time for a village was two to three years, market surveys and econometric techniques would be used to predict demand two or three years into the future to determine when to start construction of the next village.

The plan predicted the impact of development on the regional economy and tax revenues. It was expected that the state government would receive $108 million from sales and income taxes over fifteen years, Charleston County would receive $47 million from property taxes, and the local school district would receive $84,000 in 1976 alone; the overall contribution to the state's economy was predicted to be more than $1 billion in fifteen years.

Meanwhile, Sea Pines was encountering financial difficulties with its own resort and real estate operations on Hilton Head Island and elsewhere. The market for luxury recreational real estate turned way down in 1973 and 1974 as interest rates shot up, mortgage money became scarce, and overbuilding created a supply glut. Sea Pines' revenues were not enough to cover even the interest payments, which were running up to 17 percent a year, on its huge debt. The company was forced into a vast retrenchment. Much of its property was sold off, and more than 80 percent of the staff members associated with the development of new resorts were let go. Some of them ended up on the payroll of Kiawah Island Company, where the staff grew to sixty-eight. James Light, a Harvard M.B.A. whom Fraser had brought into Sea Pines in 1968, was made president of Sea Pines, although Fraser remained chairman and 49 percent stockholder.

Major opposition to the Kiawah Island development began to emerge in the summer of 1974 as environmentalists voiced fears that the island's ecological system would be destroyed. Starting in June, a spate of letters to the editor appeared arguing that the island should be left undisturbed, turned into a national seashore or a state game preserve, or opened to use by all citizens. A young man named Ben Gibbs, who had dropped out of college in 1973 to work for the former owners as a caretaker and surveyor on the island, was interviewed on national television. He said he did not like the people who were taking over the island. Immediately after the interview he either quit or was fired. The environmentalists began talking of trying to block Kiawah Island Company's application to the Charleston County Council for a zoning change to permit multiple dwelling units. Some letter writers objected to the fact that it was Arab capital and oil money doing the developing, but very few mentioned this issue.

Frank Brumley appeared before businessmen's groups, city and county agencies, environmentalists, and any other citizens who cared to hear him, patiently explaining the development plans for Kiawah. He stressed the economic benefits that would flow from the project and the precautions being taken to safeguard the ecology of the island and the welfare of nearby citizens. He made efforts to answer every charge raised and promised to modify the plans where feasible according to citizens' wishes. He quickly scotched rumors that the Arabs were planning to import camels to Kiawah and to build buildings with an Arabian motif.

The developers had their supporters too: a number of letter writers and the Charleston newspaper editors stressed the economic benefits and new jobs to be derived from the huge investment. The construction itself would require millions of dollars worth of labor and supplies from local sources. When the resort units were ready for occupancy, they would draw wealthy visitors from many states around. The resort operations and support services would provide many continuing jobs suitable for poorly educated and underprivileged residents of Charleston County, many of whom were unemployed. The benefits to the county and state tax rolls were also stressed.

Another dispute was brewing between Kiawah Island Company and Charles Fraser concerning whether Sea Pines was performing its obligations under the development contract. Williamson claimed that Sea Pines was not making available all the staff and services that were supposed to be supplied under the $100,000 monthly payment. He pointed out that Sea Pines had cut down its staff drastically under its retrenchment program and that many of those same people were fully salaried employees of Kiawah Island Company. He claimed that fewer than 50 people were available, although the contract had called for some 250. He charged in addition that Fraser had done away with the computer on which all the economic forecasting, demand prediction, budget and financing models, and the like were supposed to have been run. He began urging Kuwait Investment Company to cancel or renegotiate Kiawah Island Company's contract with Sea Pines. However, the Kuwaitis wanted Kiawah Island to be a "showpiece of Arab investment" in the United States, and so (according to Williamson) the status, prestige, and good neighborliness of the project were at least as important as its profitability. They opposed canceling the Sea Pines contract because they were afraid it would create a bad image for future Arab ventures in the U.S. They did agree that it should be renegotiated, however.

By September Sea Pines was bankrupt in all but name. On September 30, James Light met in Atlanta with the creditors, some twenty banks. He asked them to extend the loans, reduce the interest rates, and refinance $9 million of debt in order to provide two years' operating capital. The creditors reluctantly came up with $2.4 million because they believed that keeping the existing management afloat was the only possible way the company might be turned around. One factor helping persuade them to lend even this much was their knowledge that Sea Pines was receiving regular monthly payments from the Kiawah Island contract. Light said the meeting "amounted to bankruptcy court. . . . They really put us on the skewer." Fraser did not attend the meeting, but related that Light told him

> that it had been a very interesting and stormy meeting, that the creditors at that meeting were of the opinion that the Sea Pines Company in the preceding six months had been devoting an immense amount of its top level management energy to getting Kiawah Island under way, to planning the zoning campaigns, that we were focusing our attention on Kiawah Island instead of . . . our other properties, and that we should ask the Kuwait Investment Company to participate with them in a financial lending program to our company in view of our heavy focus on Kiawah Island in the preceding six months.

While Light was meeting with the bank creditors, Fraser was trying to persuade the Kuwait Investment Company to put some money into Sea Pines. He traveled first to Washington and then to Kuwait for a series of meetings with Abdlatif al Hamad and Bader al Dawood. The Kuwaitis accorded him great hospitality and showed much interest in the problems of Kiawah Island Company, particularly the zoning controversy, but in the end they turned down Fraser's request for a loan to Sea Pines.

Meanwhile the development contract between Sea Pines and Kiawah Island Company was being renegotiated. The fixed monthly payment was cut in half—to $50,000—and the services it was supposed to cover were spelled out in greater detail. Kiawah Island took over the contract for computer services so it could be assured of the use of the forecasting models and budgeting programs originally supplied by Sea Pines.

The zoning battle was shaping up into a major confrontation. In November 1974 the Charleston chapters of the National Audubon Society and the Sierra Club announced that they would seek to make Kiawah Island into a National Seashore. A group of environmentalists sent a telegram to the Sheik of Kuwait asking him to halt development until the environmental impact could be more thoroughly studied. Political candidates for local offices took stands for or against development by Kiawah Island Company, while Frank Brumley promised that the island's marshes would be protected to the "nth degree." South Carolina's outgoing governor had the idea that he might persuade the Kuwaitis to guarantee South Carolina's petroleum supply in exchange for the state's dropping all opposition to the development.

Kiawah Island Company submitted a six-volume proposal to the Charleston County Planning Board in December requesting a change in zoning from "general agricultural" to "planned unit development" (also called "planned district development"). In line with the "planned unit" concept, the proposal outlined which areas would be preserved as forest and which would be allowed for single-family units, multiple-dwelling units, or commercial use. When accepted by the county planning board and county council, the proposal would become the zoning ordinance for the district. The planning board voted unanimously to give preliminary approval to the proposal that same December, and the following month Kiawah Island Company began carving Kiawah Parkway through the forest and broke ground for the inn.

The environmentalists and other opponents were just gearing up to fight against approval by the entire county council. They incorporated a nonprofit group called the Kiawah Defense Fund and set about raising money and drumming up support. The group hired a lawyer named Frank Epstein who had earned a reputation as a civil rights activist. The group collected some 4,000 signatures of Charleston County residents on petitions opposing development by January 1975, in spite of the environmentalists' complaints that supporters of development were ripping petition forms down. Despite the signatures, Epstein realized that the number of people and the amount of money that could be raised for a purely environmental crusade were quite limited, so he determined to seek local and national allies. The national headquarters of the Audubon Society and the Sierra Club gave a little support. The environmentalists figured that they might get some support from the black subsistence farmers on nearby Johns Island. But it soon became apparent that the blacks supported the development as long as they could negotiate enough economic benefits for themselves. When news stories appeared in February about the Kuwaitis' and other Arabs' boycott of Jewish-owned banking houses in Europe, Epstein figured that Charleston's Jewish community might join the antidevelopment coalition. In fact, some of the younger Jews of Charleston, led by Rabbi Charles Sherman, did join the campaign against the Kuwaitis. But the older, more established Jewish community was cautious; they wanted to avoid irritating their Gentile neighbors, and they thought the blacks were anti-Semitic.

The environmentalist-Jewish campaign against development attracted national attention. Major American and even British newspapers ran stories on the fact that Arab money was being used to purchase and develop American real estate. Some stories criticized the Kuwaitis for putting so much money into a wealthy country like the United States rather than using it to help other less-developed countries. Senator Daniel Inouye, a Democrat from Hawaii and chairman of the Senate Foreign Commerce Subcommittee, called for an investigation. (As early as the previous September he had warned: "I don't suppose the South Carolinians watching this are too happy about having foreigners buying up their land.") In early 1975 he started hearings at which a good deal of anti-Arab testimony was heard.

The Kuwaitis were distressed at the national publicity given to the Kiawah opposition. They believed that they were receiving bad press from the *New York Times, Washington Post,* and CBS television. The Kuwaiti press criticized the Kuwait Investment Company for getting involved in the environmental dispute. On one of his regular visits to Kiawah, Adnan al Fulaij stated: "We've caught more hell in Kuwait about this than in the United States."

Meanwhile Frank Brumley was energetically shoring up supporters for the project. For months he had been making the rounds of South Carolina business and community organizations giving talks and slide shows about the development. He tailored his presentation to his audience: to Charleston businessmen he talked about the influx of tourist and resort business; to Johns Island blacks he promised a training program to prepare them for the construction and service jobs the development would open up; to county politicians he talked about the increase in the tax rolls. When environmentalists expressed fears that outdoor lighting on the beachfront houses would scare away giant seagoing loggerhead turtles from one of their last beaches for egg-laying, he had Kiawah Island Company take over funding of a study of the turtles being conducted by a University of South Carolina group. Members of the county council were given a tour of the island so they could be shown the developers' plans; rumors circulated that they were lavishly wined and dined. Brumley also invited about twenty Sierra Club members on a conducted tour. According to a club member, the visit began with "strained geniality" but deteriorated into a confrontation in the face of persistent sharp questioning by the young ex-employee Ben Gibbs. When Gibbs brought up the subject of "oil money," Brumley retorted, "The Kuwaitis have put $20 million into this development so far. Nobody walks away from $20 million, no matter how much oil they're pumping out of the ground." Brumley also moved to head off Jewish opposition by going to the office of Jack Brickman, an attorney who was the chairman of the Jewish Community Relations Committee, and discussing the possibility of a nondiscrimination pledge by Kiawah Island Company. It took a while to work out wording suitable to both Brickman and Brumley, but the pledge was eventually forthcoming.

Kiawah Island Company was making substantial efforts to preserve the island's natural environment to the greatest extent possible. This was not merely to placate the local environmentalists, Williamson said; it was also good business to protect the island's beauty in order to maintain the high selling price of the units. The company's environmentalist was working on plans to ensure low levels of electric light in the beachfront areas: "We're spending $20,000 a year on turtles," said Williamson. They were also working out ways to protect the island's deer and alligators, and several endangered species of wild birds. Any thought of hunting on the island was ruled out by Adnan al Fulaij on one of his periodic visits. "You will not harm the little things on Kiawah," he flatly ordered.

In addition to the wildlife, the geologic structure was to be protected. On the ocean front above the high-tide mark were two or three rows of sand dunes that helped protect the island's interior from strong ocean winds; the grasses and weeds on the dunes helped hold them in place and also prevented the beach from receding as its sands were swept out to sea. Leveling off these dunes would have provided a more dramatic view of the beach from the shorefront houses, but the company decided against bringing in the bulldozers. They even built wooden walkways over the dunes so that beachgoers would not wear down the sands by walking on them. "We're trying hard to do everything right," said Brumley. All of these efforts were costly; the management committee said they were fortunate to have the financial

backing of the Kuwait Investment Company in order to be
able to afford everything. They were also thankful for the
Kuwaitis' determination to make the development into a
showpiece.

Apparently the majority of public opinion as well as that
of the county council never wavered significantly from support for the development. The Charleston newspapers began
calling the Sierra and Audubon activists "ultra-environmen-
talists." The *News and Courier* editorialized:

> A trouble with the "ultras" is that they tend to muddy the waters
> of debate. They tend to create resentment against sensible, prac-
> tical environmentalists whose arguments consider human needs
> as well as those of nature. . . . The Kiawah Beach Company . . .
> has advertised its aims well in advance, accepted criticism, sto-
> ically if not always cheerfully, and modified plans according to
> public demand.

The Jews had split into factions. The younger activist
group led by Rabbi Sherman and lawyer Epstein seemed to
regard the Kiawah campaign as a crusade against the entire
Arab boycott of Israel. Some of them apparently thought
they could use Kiawah as a lever to persuade Arab countries
to modify the boycott. But the activist group failed to
gather support from the national Jewish organizations,
while the more established members of Charleston's Jewish
community seemed happy to settle for the antidiscrimination
pledge.

The Johns Island blacks were getting their benefits without
having to band together with the antidevelopers. Kiawah
Island Company promised to deposit $200,000 into a credit
union sponsored by a community group for black entrepreneurs and community organizations. There were also
rumors that the blacks' acquiescence was being purchased
by under-the-table payments.

Backers of development lined up a statement of support
from J. Mendel Davis, the U.S. congressman who repre-

sented Charleston County and who purported to speak for all six South Carolina congressmen on the issue. Fraser also arranged for Gerald Parsky, an assistant secretary of the U.S. Treasury, to telephone the county council chairman, Dr. Durst, on the day a public meeting was to be held on the zoning variance. Parsky advised Durst that the federal government favored a policy of allowing free trade and investment across all national borders. (Opponents later protested that the federal government was interfering in what should be a local government matter, and one went so far as to telephone Parsky the next day to clarify his remarks. Parsky and Durst both denied there was any attempt to pressure the county council's decision.)

The antidevelopment campaign came to a head at a March 24 public meeting, which had to be moved from its original location to the county library because of the anticipated crowd. An overflow crowd of 350 to 450 people came in spite of rain and the threat of a hurricane; more than 100 people were denied admission to the meeting room because of lack of seating space. Conservationists and Jewish groups picketed outside with signs reading "Americans Yes! Kuwaitis No!" and "Keep Kiawah American!" Each side—the proponents of the zoning variance and their opponents—was granted seventy-five minutes speaking time. Speaking for the proposal, Frank Brumley said that the company could subdivide the entire island under its existing "general agricultural" classification, but that they would be limited to one-family dwellings. He made it clear that the company would take this route if it was forced to, but argued that it would be less attractive than erecting a limited number of multiple-occupancy units with large areas of forest preserved around them. Opponents of the variance engaged in a certain amount of hyperbole: Epstein said it "would completely destroy the maritime forests," and another speaker said it would "amount to a blank check surrounded by the most minimal protection." The most emotional objections came from Jewish speakers, many of whom referred to Arab attempts to boycott U.S. firms doing business with Israel. Rabbi Sherman said: "America's blood was shed and flowed so that no country could take by force what the Arabs would take with oil money."

On April 10 the council voted unanimously to grant the variance and permit Kiawah Island to be developed as a planned development district. This was essentially the end of the zoning battle but not the end of unfavorable national publicity about Kiawah Island. In April in a syndicated newspaper column titled "Sheiks Plan Rich Spa in South Carolina," investigative reporter Jack Anderson reported: "The Kuwaitis have chosen Sea Pines Corp., a company accused of subtle prejudice against Jews, to develop and manage the posh island resort. . . . A former high-level employee charged that Sea Pines' salesmen were told by their bosses, 'We don't have any Jews here (at Hilton Head). We want the Jews to stay in Miami.' " A few days later the Charleston *Evening Post,* under the headline "Anderson Had It All Wrong, Fraser Says," reported: "The simple fact is there have been a large number of Jewish guests who keep coming back to Sea Pines Plantation."

Apparently the reportage was having some effect on other Arab observers. The commercial attaché at the Saudi Arabian embassy in Washington, D.C., was quoted as saying that Saudi investments do not include real estate: "The Kuwaitis have some, Kiawah Island, but they are sorry they did it. They have received too much bad publicity." An American businessman who returned to the United States after five years in Kuwait added that Arabs were afraid that if the political climate went against them in this country, their investments might be nationalized and they would end up with nothing.

The Kuwaitis and their American managers assessed the position of Kiawah Island Company in January 1976. Kuwait Investment had put almost $36 million into the purchase and development of the island and knew its development was

attractive. The investment company was of course financially
strong, and could afford to ride out a slow start in sales. The
Kuwaitis, however, were tiring of plowing ever more money
into the project when they had no way of knowing whether
it would finally sell. There were three competing resort developments within a 100-mile radius (including Sea Pines Plantation on Hilton Head Island). The United States was just coming out of its severest and longest recession since the Great
Depression, and the housing and construction industries had
been the hardest hit of all. Kiawah Island had received a lot
of unfavorable publicity over the environmental and Jewish
issues, which might have the effect of turning off prospective
buyers. Some American commentators had shown nationalis-
tic reactions against the Arab owners. And the Sea Pines contract, which had earlier been seen as a blessing, had now
become a $50,000-per-month liability, a huge potential
claim on future profits, and an albatross around the company's neck. The press and the public back in Kuwait were
quite critical of the investment company for entering the
project in the first place, particularly in view of the expense,
bad publicity, and uncertain returns. In these circumstances,
the Kuwaiti investors and their American managers could
only pray that sales of the lots and houses would be strong
and occupancy of the inn high.

In February 1976 Kiawah Island Company notified Sea
Pines that it was terminating the development contract on
the grounds that Sea Pines had been in default for more than
a month. Shortly thereafter Kuwait Investment filed suit for
damages, claiming that Sea Pines had failed to provide certain services specified in the contract and had shifted expenses
such as employees' salaries onto Kiawah Island Company.
Sea Pines filed a counterclaim charging that Kuwait Investment terminated the contract just when the development
was completed and profits were expected. (Fraser commented
that Bader al Dawood, who had replaced Abdlatif al Hamad
as president of Kuwait Investment, had "gotten cute" and

decided to terminate just when they had received all the benefits from Sea Pines and would avoid sharing the profits.) Sea
Pines took the publicity offensive with a news conference,
in which James Light said the Kuwaitis' suit was "an undis-
guised attempt to squeeze us out of the project. . . . If they
break faith with their partner, then I can't predict how they
will handle their other commitments."

In early May, just as Kiawah was opening up for business,
the Sunday paper carried a feature story, "Arab Nations Eye
Kiawah's Progress." It reported:

> Kuwait and other Middle Eastern countries "are waiting to see
> what is the result of Kiawah and an $85 million hotel complex
> in Atlanta before developing future investment plans," said
> Mohammed Y. al Qatami, a young Kuwaiti who is a member of
> the Kuwait Investment Company board of directors. "The
> Kuwait expenditures on Kiawah indicate the confidence the
> Kuwaitis have in the U.S. economy." The economy soured during
> early development, but the Kuwait investors continued to pump
> money derived from its vast oil resources into the project. . . .
> Qatami declined to discuss national or international politics or
> the litigation between Kuwait Investment Co. and Sea Pines
> Company.

A successor article, titled "Kuwait Investors All Business,"
related that

> during construction, Kuwait representatives regularly made the
> 22-hour, 7,000-mile trip from their tiny sheikdom to view prog-
> ress at Kiawah. Their arrivals and departures were cloaked in
> secrecy. They did not want public attention. "We are business
> people," said Mohammed Y. al Qatami. . . . "We are not interested
> in attention."

The paper described the Kuwaitis as "smiling and courteous
. . . conservatively dressed . . . reluctant about being interviewed."

Richard Williamson resigned from his job as investment
advisor to the Kuwait Investment Company in June 1976

and returned to a job at the University of South Carolina. Fraser believed the reason he resigned was because his relations with Bader al Dawood had become strained.

Kiawah Island facilities began opening to the public in summer 1976. The inn, restaurants, public beach, shopping mall, and golf course all rapidly became popular. Sales of lots, condominiums, and the dozen or so beachfront houses officially opened in August. Within two months the paper reported: "Kiawah Sales Booming: Kiawah Island Company has sold 140 of 180 lots in a real estate sales boom that puts the company one year ahead of its own projections." By January 1977 it was reported in an article titled "Resort Island Results Win Lowcountry Approval":

> Murmurs of apprehension three years ago over the Kuwaiti "invasion" of Charleston County have turned into gestures of affection. . . . The Kiawah development resulted in $12.4 million in sales during the first 7½ months. . . . Brumley said the success of Kiawah can be attributed . . . most importantly to its "solid financial ownership. People don't have to be concerned that the developer may be gone tomorrow."

At the time of this writing Kiawah Island Company and Sea Pines were still skirmishing over legal technicalities and were unwilling to discuss what negotiations were taking place toward settlement of the lawsuits.

Bibliography

Adams, Michael, ed. *The Middle East: A Handbook.* New York: Praeger, 1971.

American University, Foreign Area Studies Division. *Area Handbook for Iran.* U.S. Government Printing Office, 1971. (Area handbooks are also available for most of the countries of the Middle East.)

Amirsadeghi, Hossein, ed. *Twentieth Century Iran.* New York: Hornes and Meier, 1977.

Anthony, John Duke. *Arab States of the Lower Gulf: People, Politics and Petroleum.* Washington, D.C.: The Middle East Institute, 1975.

Berque, Jacques. *Cultural Expression in Arab Society Today.* Austin: University of Texas Press, 1976.

Bill, James Alban. *The Politics of Iran: Groups, Classes and Modernization.* Columbus, Ohio: Charles E. Merrill Publishing Company, 1972.

Fayerweather, John and Kapoor, Ashok. *Strategy and Negotiation for the International Corporation.* Cambridge, Mass.: Ballinger Press, 1976.

Fenelon, K. G. *The United Arab Emirates: An Economic and Social Survey.* London: Longman, 1976.

Haim, Sylvia, ed. *Arab Nationalism.* Berkeley: University of California Press, 1962.

Khadduri, Majid. *Political Trends in the Arab World: The Role of Ideas and Ideals in Politics.* Baltimore: Johns Hopkins Press, 1970.

Khouin, Nounah A. and Algar, Hamid, eds. and trans. *An Anthology of Modern Arabic Poetry.* Berkeley: University of California Press, 1976.

Kritzeck, James. *Modern Islamic Literature.* New York: Mentor Books, 1972.

Lenckzowski, George, ed. *Political Elites in the Middle East.* Washington, D.C.: American Enterprise Institute, 1975.

Lewis, Bernard, ed. *Islam.* New York: Harper & Row, 1974.

Mansfield, Peter, ed. *The Middle East: A Political and Economic Survey.* London: Oxford University Press, 1973.

Nutting, Anthony. *The Arabs.* New York: New American Library, 1964.

Operating in Iran: An Economic Coming of Age. Business International Research Report, New York, 1978.

Pearson, Robert P. *Through Middle Eastern Eyes.* New York: Praeger, 1975.

Udovitch, A. L., ed. *The Middle East: Oil, Conflict and Hope.* Lexington, Mass.: Heath, 1976.

U.N. Joint Conference on Trade and Development. *Joint Ventures Among Developing Countries: Arab Countries.* Prepared by Ibrahim F. I. Shihata, consultant.

Wickersham, Warren J. and Fishburne, Benjamin P., III, eds. *Current Legal Aspects of Doing Business in the Middle East: Saudi Arabia, Egypt and Iran.* Washington, D.C.: American Bar Association, 1977.

Zonis, Marvin. *The Political Elite of Iran.* Princeton: Princeton University Press, 1971.